ANCHOR BOOKS

OUR NATURAL WORLD

Edited by

David Foskett

First published in Great Britain in 1996 by
ANCHOR BOOKS
1-2 Wainman Road, Woodston,
Peterborough, PE2 7BU

HB ISBN 1 85930 378 1
SB ISBN 1 85930 373 0

Foreword

Anchor Books is a small press, established in 1992, with the aim of promoting readable poetry to as wide an audience as possible.

We hope to establish an outlet for writers of poetry who may have struggled to see their work in print.

The poems presented here have been selected from many entries. Editing proved to be a difficult and daunting task and as the Editor, the final selection was mine.

The wonderful world of nature is all around us, with its many hidden wonders. Just take a close look for yourself and you will see.

All the poets included in this beautiful collection, have taken the time to stand back and take in the many sights and sounds of nature, to produce this relaxing anthology of verse.

Take a quiet spot in the open air and be prepared to take a trip into the wild outdoors and discover the many beauty spots we tend to take for granted.

I trust this selection will delight and please the authors and all those who enjoy reading poetry.

David Foskett
Editor

CONTENTS

THE GARDEN OF GOD

Flowers of many colours
In God's garden grow
Living waters trickle
Rivulets a-flow
Golden sunshine glorious
Where night and stars have been
Jigsaw pieces fitting
To make a happy scene!

Mary Hayworth

GREEN LAND

Milk bottles on the bank,
Everywhere I go -
I see crisp packets . . .
Crumpled and crinkled.

Rubbish in gardens,
Nappies -
Sweet wrappers . . .
Oh no!
Cleaning up time.

The world should be clean!
Every path I walk . . . dogs toilet!
Riding on my bike -
Through my tyres it goes . . .
Splish!

Walking with my dog
Through the green grass,
Wet and sloshy . . . nice and straight;
Daffodils out . . . pretty flowers -
Rubbish? . . . Nowhere!

Christina Lewis (9)

CROWDED OUT

Tussocked fields,
Fly-shadowed cows,
Tasselled tails flicking.
Hedging hawthorns
Flower heaped:
Creamy milkshake
Pinks, and white.

Conker-shiny
Grumbling
Chicken
Stab, scratch,
Scuttle freely.
This field
House-hemmed.

Before too long
Snaky streets,
Human housefuls,
Will stretch,
Gobble.
Eat up fields,
Chicken, cows.

Felicity M Bradley

BLIND MAN

Full of pride and vanity
Man struts the earth,
He boasts of his achievements,
Whilst all uncaring
With unseeing eyes
He is surrounded by
The master's work day by day . . .

Florence Andrews

GO GREEN ONLY TO BE SEEN

So you say that you are green,
But it's only so you can be seen.
To care for this earth God did make,
It's not really for the people's sake.
You save paper, bottles and cans,
Then you go and blow off hands.
With land mines that make you money,
Millions starving, yet you live on honey.
You who have all the real power,
Will sell arms to all, at any hour.
But you have a respectable face,
Dress your child in silk and lace.
True you're green as green can be,
Unless it cuts your profits I see.
You're a real environmentally friendly guy,
Only now and then do you pollute the sky.
You only bury low level radiation things,
They're not too harmful to human beings.
I know you do deadly secret deals,
Selling electric stun batons to those who feel,
That their victim deserves a little prod,
When his government gives him the nod.
You say you're green as green can be,
But you live in Britain and you are free.

Don Goodwin

AN APOLOGY

Sorry brown cow very sorry indeed
Although you could be any colour or breed
How much better it would have been
If only you had grazed on the grass so green.

Sorry brown cow you had no voice or say
Perhaps if you had there would be no BSE today
One wonders why this food was conceived
It seemed just the right way to spread disease.

Sorry brown cow when you were such a success
That man created for you such distress
You gave us calves, milk all the year round
Yet for you no cure have they found.

Sorry brown cow mad cow disease it was called
That cannot be right when man was the cause
Chickens were fed in much the same way
The hardship it made is still with us today.

Sorry brown cow it seems man cannot learn
For common sense we should yearn
It should not have happened! Not to you.
If man's not careful he could catch it too.

A D Mason

GREEN LEAF AND BLUE WATER

Trees, grass, flowers
earth, sea, sky
calling waters
the whispering breeze
sun, moon, stars

All these . . . all these . . .

Louise Rogers

SAVE OUR SEAS

I am an aquanaut
Many hours a week I spend in the sea
My piscean companions
Mean the world to me
The atrocities I find there
You could not comprehend
I swim with friendly fishes
In rocky terrain and sand
Monsters in human form
Corrupt and poison them
Foolish as they have become
Harvest them and eat them
Feed them to their innocent offspring
A perfect conclusion succinct
A sure fire solution if he could bring
The end become extinct
Leave our sub-aqua world alone
How much more must my friends suffer
Through man's gross ignorance
Cloned greedy perpetuator's mutter
How long before
Man destroys himself his seed
Make peace not war
Let us try again to get it right
Were you to see the trusting eye
See their soul hear their sigh
You would surely voice their silent pleas
To save our suffering seas

Margareth

NEW BYPASS

The striding new bypass
Cannot see
The country disappear
So quickly.

The child's hand
Travelling at speed
And put out from
A car's window

May no longer
Hold another hand

To save its life.

Andrew Baily

SEASONS AND BIRDS

January sees the shelduck sitting in a rabbit burrow
February a little owl swoops over open countryside
In March, the kingfisher rests at the waterside
And April brings a bluetit to perch on leafless hazel twigs

In May, a yellowhammer comes hopping through
Blackthorn hedgerows
And June is when swallows fly home from South Africa
July, and the bullfinch enjoys eating soft fruits
In August, wrens flit through tangled twigs to search for insects

September and the jay collects acorns to bury in the ground for winter
And October the waxwing from north Europe gorges on berries
In November, we see the great spotted woodpecker,
Drumming his beak for all to hear
And in December, we see our favourite Christmas card bird,
The robin, who hunts for worms in our gardens.

J M Stoles

SPRINGTIME, THE WORLD ABOUT US

How lovely is the springtime,
With sunshine and with rain,
The wintertime is over,
We see the flowers again.

The daffodils are nodding,
With bonnets on their heads,
The hyacinths and tulips,
Have risen from their beds.

Honey bees are waking up,
Pollen from the flowers they seek,
While high up in the tall yew trees,
The rooks have built their nest.

See over the upland and lowland,
The charm of a lovely spring day,
With bluebells and primroses sweet,
While children and dogs in gardens play.

Baby lambs when dawn is breaking,
Dance around their mother sheep,
While the hedgehogs are yawning,
Waking up from their winter deep.

We may gather the sweet wild flowers,
From hedgerows and shady lanes,
The skylarks they will rise and sing,
Joining the chorus when church bells ring.

Yes, nature is here to greet us,
With colour and birds on the wing,
Just beautiful are the scenes around us,
When happy sunlight fills each day of spring.

Hilary Vickers

ALAS FOR POOR NATURE

Alas for poor nature,
It treated us well,
Fruit to eat,
And trees to fell.
Nature provided,
For young and for old,
With furs for our backs,
For when we were cold.
Nature was silent,
When we wanted rest,
And music provided,
From birds in their nests.
Nature made everything,
For man to possess,
And gave it up willingly,
And never did rest.
Now look how we treat it,
For all it has gave,
We cut down whole forests,
We make it a slave.
We should all help,
To maintain nature's grace,
And not to destroy it,
Just to make space;
For houses and factories -
A demand we must meet,
While smothering nature,
With dark grey concrete.
Now we all know,
The trouble we're in,
The colours of nature,
Are faded and dim.

Some try to restore them,
But the colours are gone,
Destroyed now forever -
By what man has done.

A W Kennedy

BLOOMS OF NATURE

As I walk down memory lane
 I can visualise my children in the rain
Picking daffodils for Mother's Day
 This way nature provides, they've saved
their pay.

With my children I've admired the view
 Of springtime flowers screaming out with
contrasting colours anew
 They wave, they dance, and blow, I sneeze
The pollen count must be up, I'm beginning
 to wheeze.

The colour of a daffodil, warms my day
 Red and purple crocuses are patriotic
in some way
 While orange and green are natural
colours in the sun
 They compliment the beauty of everyone.

It's a pity the flowers' lives are short
 'A lot of effort's put in growing them
That I will support'.
 Thank goodness for the gardening
skills
 And the council's efforts, in paying
the bills.

Margaret Jowsey

COLOURS OF CHANGE

If the sky was green,
Just think of what it would look like.
If the rivers were red,
Where would the fish swim.
Think if the grass was blue,
How would you react.
Blue is just a colour,
But it's not the colour of grass.

Why do we want to change.
Are we not happy,
With what we have.

Anthony Bowler

LOST REFLECTION

There upon the water danced
Raindrops in delighted glee,
Obscuring all reflections
That have inspired me.

But, as I watched, I smiled,
The raindrops oe'er the lake,
As, reflection they defiled,
Their dance like imps at play

The bracken coloured water
Rejoiced at their delight,
And gathered them like children
Before the coming night.

I glanced at nearby silver birch,
with raindrops all arrayed
Along her purple branches gleam,
Such beauty from the rain.

Jean Mackereth

JUDGEMENT ON THE HUMAN APHIDS

If only we could stand back and see
That we are global garden pests,
The ones who kill the beneficial plants.
Perhaps before it is too late the
Gardener will come and spray us all.

Rosa Barbary

HOW VALERIE, THE OFFICE DOG'S-BODY, MET A SQUIRREL

The photocopier jammed again today.
I'm the office junior,
the dog's-body, so it's my job to fix it.
When I opened it up and a squirrel jumped out,
I knew it wasn't the usual problem.

Inside the machine all the paper,
thousands of sheets,
had turned green and taken root.
It smelled like a compost heap.
I was elbow deep in loam.
Gone, the plastic and the chrome,
the steel cogs and rubber wheels.
Gone, all that clever-clever machinery.
In its place?
Forest, as far as my eye could see.
Just then the boss called out,
'Fixed it yet, Valerie?'
'Not quite,' I said, 'I think it's a job for a chain-saw . . . '
'Valerie!' he barked, 'just fix it will you!
I don't pay you to be funny. Remember: time's money.'

Chris Culshaw

A WINTER WHITE-OUT

These harshest of winds, like a cat o' nine tails,
lashing our world with sleet, snow and hail.
Stooping in fear, boughs creak and groan,
at war with the elements, a battle zone.
Blizzards sweep and swirl in furious rage,
a mighty force transforming an image.
Blotting out landscapes with apparent ease,
haphazard drifting completes the disguise.
Enslavement within its vicious power,
minions trapped in their ivory towers.
A Siberian winter, 'From Russia with love',
the roar of a wild beast not the sound of a dove.

Sheelagh Evans

A BUTTERFLY

I see a butterfly fluttering across the lawn
And stare at it flitting here and there
How delicate, fragile and transient it is
Its myriad colours dazzling in the sunlight
It lands briefly on the blossoming rose
Bringing instant joy deep into my heart
Its graceful wings flapping endlessly
Giving immediate pleasure to my senses
Should I sing reverence to Mother Nature
For showing me wonderful and glorious beauty
The butterfly lasted a short time in my vision
Yet it filled me with an ephemeral loveliness
Such a wondrous thing I will behold in my mind
And I will remember always the joy I received.

Luciene Azique

CYCLES

Buds breaking out
like measles' spots on childish skin.
Slowly opening
just as child-like hand unfurls.

Leaves open wide
searching for sunlight.
Canopy is arrayed,
beauty more than a girl's first gown.

Colour changes now
red, gold, brown, autumnal shades.
Wind blows leaves to ground,
trees as in twilight years.

Twigs, branches bare
having lost the bloom of life.
Life ebbing slowly
as in later years of man.

Winter, cold, icy,
Trees, naked, as in death.
Await the warmth of spring,
resurrection, as life anew.

Trees, man, life,
such is the cycle.
Entwined through ages
Life, death, emerge as hope.

Josie Minton

REALITY

As I sit by my window,
I don't hear birds singing
or see trees swaying in
the gentle breeze.

I hear car engines,
babies crying, people shouting.
Other people's music or televisions blaring.
Children playing games.

I hear life as it is,
not as it is written.

Occasionally the birds can be heard,
Occasionally the scent of fresh air rises
up through the smog, and the leaves can be
heard rustling over the concrete mass
that rules our lives.

Fantasy fills many pages of many books.
Reality is here and now.
Reality won't be ignored.

Reality is . . . outside my bedroom
window.

A J Haughton

SPRINGTIME IN A NAME

B lossom on the trees
E arly Crocus here
V eils and veils of Snowdrops
E aster bonnets, cheer
R ows of blue Forget-Me-Nots
L ittle Lambs at play
E aster eggs and fluffy chicks
Y our beautiful spring day

Irene Corin

NATURE'S REASONS

Seasons come and seasons go
We never miss them, we always know,
We know the autumn, when leaves fall
We know the winter when Santa may call.
With spring so fresh all so new,
The summer season with skies of blue.

With every season a new sight
A different colour, a different light,
A gentle glow in an autumn sky
White winter snow crisp and dry.
Spring greens a smell so sweet,
The summer sun a warming treat.

Seasons come and seasons go,
With everyone nature will grow,
Leaves may fall, yet they'll live again
Snow soon softens in a melting rain.
Buds peep out to a fresh sun
With summer another season of fun,
For all this change, nature gives no reasons
Of why we have four different seasons.

Andrea Jay

SPRING

The buds have blossomed,
The trees grow leaves,
And daffodils are stolen,
By those impetuous thieves.

Yes once again,
We're in the season of spring,
Oh! The smiles of pleasure,
It shall bring.

New-born lambs,
Bounce happily around,
Mother ewe is content,
They're safe and sound.

Summer is only,
A few months away,
For glorious sunshine,
I do pray.

But right now I'll enjoy,
The delights that are here,
Because spring is my favourite,
Season of the year.

Catriona Kneeland (13)

THE THRUSH'S TRIUMPH

Regal visitor
perched so straight and upstanding,
proud of his white coat.
His trophy, juicy berries
snatched from the snow laden bough.

Joy Aldridge

SPRING

Oh to be young when spring is in the air
Life's full of promise, you haven't a care
The air is scented with blossoms anew
The smell of fresh grass fills the air
Daffodils nod off without a care
Walks in the park, the boat lake alive
With new baby ducklings trying to survive
Lovers stroll hand in hand
Hearts fit to burst
Hoping love will blossom
With love that is true
The world has come alive
Looking fresh and new

Irene Pearce

FUNNY THING NATURE

It's a funny thing nature
It's with us all year
And look at the changes
It suddenly appears.

It's a funny thing nature
It waits for nobody
Some call it many things
Even a hobby.

It's a funny thing nature
It works wonders too
And shapes many things
Wondrous for me and *You.*

Keith L Powell

SPRING

The sun returns from hibernation
Night gives more to day
A rainbow of green and yellow
Replaces the winter's grey

Nature awakens
From its winter rest
Life begins again
The year introduces its first guest

Bare earth becomes a garden
An explosion of fun
Daffodils dance in the gentle breeze
Encouraged by the sun

Lambs bounce in the fields
Eggs hatch into fluffy chicks
Blossom adorns the returning trees
As nature plays its tricks

We awaken to the dawn chorus
The birds now sing
Life returns with reason
The earth gives birth to spring.

Michelle Roberts

SEASONS

The woods are blue with bluebells
The sky above is clear
A thrush sings in the treetops
Announcing spring is here

We go from spring to summer
The time when holidays are spent
At home or in foreign countries
Where you laze to your content

Then it's on to autumn
And all the leaves are brown
And squirrels are looking for food
That lies upon the ground

Before you know winter's here
With holly, mistletoe and cheer
Another year has passed by
Once again there is a blue spring sky.

Jean Bradbury

SPRING

Winter wane with waxen moon, temperature will rise quite soon
Pendulous, the catkins swing, splendid, yellow, advent spring
Frost hardened ground, crumbles, moist, seed and bulb, new life they hoist
Tenderest tentacles, squirm into view, explode with springtime
resplendent hue

Crocus joined with snowdrops show, pulsing through belated snow
Small and perfect, crisp and bright, the season starts with pearled delight
Tulips form and graceful make, petals pointed, bold, opaque
Leaves uplifted cool at night, stem erect, and petalled tight

Daffodil cloistered, trumpet voluntary, music to the eyes, pure quality
Crimpled horn, triumphant raised, tribute to the season praised
Rockery stark, in winters strife, now ablaze with coloured life
Ground cover plants complete for room, alpine heather short lived bloom

Borders salute, in soldier's style, at attention transplants smile
Regimented, grouped with power, green stemmed army, parading flower
Branched trees sprouting bulbous bud, leafy sleek from last years wood
Foliage crown gargantuan, home for birds in leafy span

Height of spring on rockery slope, pristine, pastel, kaleidoscope
England's gardens fulfilled in bloom, now we forget the winter gloom

Charles B Sutton

SHADES OF EVENING

I gazed from out my window
As twilight time was nigh
The silence it was golden
Beneath the purple sky
The silhouette of a lonely fox
Appeared upon the hill
Bats swooped down on swarms of gnats
To eat their evening fill
All the shades of evening
Soon disappeared from sight
An inky black fell o'er the scene
As day turned into night

Joyce M Chaffer

SPRING-TIME

It is spring, it is spring
The birds gaily sing
While busily building a nest
It is spring, it is spring
The young lambs frisk
In the meadow
Where the mother sheep rest,
It is spring, it is spring
The trees are all budding
Every little shoot so new,
It is spring, it is spring
The hedgerows glisten
Bathed in the morning dew,
Be glad the sun shines
Be glad the birds sing
Be glad for this morning
It is spring, spring, spring.

Nora Kathleen Cooper

THE WORLD ABOUT US

When autumn days grow shorter
And light begins to fade
We know that winter's on it's way
With gloomy days of shade

But winter holds some wonderment
Winds blow with all their might
Frost turns water hard as stone
Snow changes grey to white

Ice thaws and water trickles
To fill the lakes and streams
Snow slowly melts and sun shines through
Life merges from its dreams

Buds burst from barren branches
Shoots push up through the ground
Suddenly the earth awakes
With greenness all around

Summer flowers in full bloom
Colours of every hue
The days are very long and hot
With skies of heavenly blue

Fruits and berries deck the trees
Leaves turn gold and red
Then fall like carpets over ground
To quilt earth's winter bed.

Pamela A Lower

THE SOUND OF SILENCE

In a leafy glade so quiet where
The perfume of bluebells fills the air,
I tiptoe softly on mossy leaves
Where no man walks, no roadways weaves,
And all I hear is the sound of silence.

Look! A lake of mirrored perfection where
My silhouette's a neat reflection there,
No reeds a-rustling nor waves a-lapping,
No sound from the owl on phantom wing,
Only the eerie sound of silence.

Look! My empty childhood home where
Memories force me to stand and stare,
Noises of laughter, of children singing
In my mind and ears are now ringing
Loudly, in the sound of silence.

Onward through the forest hushed where
To make one noise I would not dare,
I'm standing still and listening now
God made this haven, I know not how,
And I thank Him for this sound of silence.

Christine Farmer

NATURE'S CHILD

A top of stem, a flower's born,
As little bud begins to breathe,
Slowly upshoots into life,
Begins to dance, in morning breeze.

Unfurl of leaf to petal show,
A beauty blossom, soon to be,
With just a hint of nature shade,
All colour tints, here to see.

Away in meadow corner sits,
Betwixt the reeds and grass so tall,
Where no eyes see, can safely grow,
This wonder great that e'er be small.

If thou e'er travel to this spot,
Pluck from ground, dare thee not,
Leave it be, let it alone,
This field of grass, do be its home.

Dancer

SUMMER'S ON THE WAY

Summer's on the way, I can feel
it in the air.

The days are getting warmer, the
nights are getting lighter, yes summer's
on the way.

The hot sun shines through my
window, and birds sing their songs
in the trees.

Children play happily in the local
park, people walk their dogs and
whistle merry tunes.

Young girls sunbathe in their gardens,
young men gather to exchange the
latest news.

Yes, summer's on the way,
I can feel it in my blood.

Thank the Lord for Summer.

Garry Mitchell

OUR WORLD

Forest facing mass destruction,
wildlife hunted to extinction,
rivers stagnant with pollution,
people suffering deprivation
many dying from starvation,
children sick with radiation,
creation cries with desperation
in this world with such disruption
can there ever be salvation.

Keith Slatter

OBSERVATION

The summer sun is shining,
The birds are flying high,
The flowers exude a lovely scent,
The trees emit a sigh.
The breeze that waves the fields of corn -
The harvest mouse's home,
The stream that wanders on its way
As o'er the fields I roam.
Each blade of grass I see so clear,
The insects running round,
I've never looked so hard before
At things upon the ground.
The crying of a baby,
The cooing of a dove,
The smiling faces all around
Of all those that we love.
The trees that stand so stately tall,
The shrubs close to the ground,
All the creatures great and small
From His true love abound.

Ruth Smith

WINTER AMBIENCE

Frost laden hedgerows groan under the
weight of winter's white.
Laughing children brush past them, sending clouds
of icy powder into flight.
Hidden spider's webs now starkly revealed by the cold,
display their intricate beauty.
Bejewelled in frozen diamonds, adorning their
delicate mystery.
Snow crunching underfoot; solitary journeys imprinted
and preserved in an Arctic blanket.
All is made equal poor house or palace stand together
as icy sculptures set.
In the mystical shroud of winter's all embracing
frozen cloak.
Creating familiar Christmas card scenes with all the
warmth they evoke.
Sparkling droplets fill the chilly air, from the biting
cold there is no escape.
Distant summer brightness and autumn riches
dissipate into a fairytale landscape.
Bathed in weak winter sun, struggling to permeate
an ambient, frozen haze.
This is the magical wonderland of precious
winter days.

Joanna Malone

SPRING FEELINGS

Up early one morning
I looked through the window
Birds were singing, young seagulls
Flew around overhead
The sun was shining to herald a new day
I felt a certain feeling of elation
A feeling that Spring was here
Buds on trees and shrubs are opening
Daffodils sway gracefully in the morning breeze
Primula hold sweet faces to the morning sun
Tulips stand stately in brilliant red

I view the jobs of the day
Lawns to be cut, borders dug and tidied
Plants to be sorted, seeds in plant pots
Sorting in the garage
I fetch out the mountain bikes
All to be cleaned and oiled
Busy with dusters my imagination takes me
Through the local woods, riding over
Hills and dales, bait boxes well packed

Still dreaming, our caravan now standing
On our frontal patch
I looked at it, Spring is here I thought
I unlocked the caravan door
Stepping in, I thought of happy times
Holiday camps, old castles, fishing
The one and only foreign holiday
My happy elated feeling still persisted
I was opening up to Spring

Evelyn Ida Henfield

A DAY IN MAY

I want to tell you of a day in Spring
Bright with buttercups and cuckoo flowers,
And sweet with scent of coconut
From sun-warmed blossom on the whin;
Of skylarks high in a clear wide sky
Hovering like tiny predators
And pouring forth their hearts in endless song

The distant hills were blue as blue,
There was a rapture in the air
But oh, how could such joyous life and beauty be
Alongside sickness, suffering and despair?
Flying low, a curlew gave its haunting cry
Echoing the question in my mind,
No answer came . . .

But standing there
Amid the dunes and shining grass,
I gradually became aware
Of a Presence - known before
In time of need.
Cosmic in immensity
Personal in intensity
It wrapped me round.

And suddenly I have no words
To tell you or explain
How to a troubled anxious heart
Such strength and comfort came.

Patricia Graeme

DRY SEASON

Dry season, ground hard
arid, dusty and waterless
Gasping, dehydrated, plants parched
husky, dry as a bone
Thirsty, craving famished land
Locked in drought, seared and sapless
Heavens open, cloudburst cascade
Monsoon deluge, quenching downpour
Rivulets and runnels, gurgle and guggle
babble and bubble, dribble and trickle
Water the life giver, soaking in
Dormant grasses germinating, sprouting
spreading outwards, a sea of green
Feeding, nourishing, snatching relief
before baking desert sun returns.

Paul Birkitt

COTSWOLD SPRING

Come first of March spring buds have sprung,
Rust fields well spread with fertile dung
And larks their earliest solos sung.

The morning mists awash with dew,
And noonday skies a tremulous blue
And evening's lengthening dusky hue.

When ewes are driven to field from fold,
And wintered herds back on the wold,
The season's springtime tale is told.

And we who thrive on Cotswold air
And feel the west wind tug our hair
Are blest to know that we are there.

Maida Sturge

BLOSSOM TIME

Fragrant clouds of pink and white
Cover woodland trees.
Petals falling, twisting, twirling,
Dancing in the breeze.
Creamy spikes on chestnuts tall,
Like lighted candles glow.
Hawthorn blossoms on the hedge,
White as the driven snow.
Busy bees flit to and fro,
Butterflies take wing.
In forest glen, in woodland glade,
Joyful songbirds sing.
Against a chequered background,
Of countless shades of green,
Purple rhododendrons,
And wild lilac can be seen.
Warming rays of sunshine,
Morning dew and rain,
Wakes each bud from winter's sleep,
And bids them bloom again.
Honeysuckle twines the bough,
With the dog rose sweet,
The forest blossoms into life,
When spring and nature meet.

Jenny Porteous

NIGHTSTORM

'Tis at night, whilst warm in your bed,
the storm begins, with the wind driven rain.
it arrives hard, at each and every window pane.
Then, for a brilliant, time splitting second,
the lightning creases, and splits up the sky.

Again, more lightning flashes, one by one,
as the thunder roars and crashes,
across the brilliant, then blackened sky.
All jerk awake, with the ghost like flashes
and extend an ear, listening with an open eye.

Everything is sound, creaks, groans and wind howling,
then, when well aware of sounds below stair,
a night of well being, no dogs are growling.
The storm, driving rain and turbulent air,
causes everyone to snuggle deep, not caring.

There are those, whose duties, demand night work,
who will be driving, or walking into the downpour.
Who knows of the Paramedics, Firemen, brought out,
as firebells go down, a house hit, or more.
As forked lightning strikes, natures energy bout.

For me like everyone, here on Mother Earth
the conflicts of climate, are something we must bear.
Now how many of us have said, in a moment of mirth,
because, come a stormy night, who really does care.
When you can slide luxuriously into sleep, deep in your berth.

Alan Noble

NATURE'S HARMONY

Every morning the sun will rise
Every evening set,
Although we may not always see
We depend upon this yet.

Every spring the flowers bloom
Blossoms burst anew
The trees in leaf, reborn,
Grass bespecked with dew.

Each time the summer comes around
With sun for warmth and play,
Holidays and leisure time
To end a working day.

Every autumn, harvesting
Fields of ripening grain,
Nuts, and fruits and berries
Gathered in again.

Every night the stars appear
The moon rises, above
Eternal gifts of light,
God's legacy of love.

So give thanks and praise to God above
For stars and sun and moon,
As all the changing seasons play
Nature's harmonic tune.

Joan Heybourn

TRAVELLING

I have travelled with the wind
O'er mountain tops, through forest glades.
Recalling times that might have been
As all too soon those memories fade.

I have travelled with the rain
Lashing down on earth below.
Watching swinging weather vanes
Twisting, turning to and fro.

I have travelled with the sun
O'er deserts hot and burnished beaches.
Caught it when the day is done
Or its fiery zenith reaches.

I have travelled with the earth
Merrymaking, feet a tapping.
Burdens lightened, joy and mirth
Fireflies in a landscape dancing.

I have travelled with all these things
Elements of life, so fine
Bliss or sorrow to each they bring
Yet the promise of rewards divine.

Eileen Laura Gregson

SONNET FOR SPRING

The naked earth lies bare and brown at last,
Its snowy blanket melted into dew;
The arctic nights are thankfully long past,
And Nature's yearly cycle starts anew.

The snowdrop stands, a herald of the spring,
A slender sign that winter's day is done;
The linnets and the larks again take wing,
And crocuses glow golden in the sun.

A welcome warmth engenders hope once more,
Unlocking frozen hearts and leaden skies;
The curlew's heard above the torrent's roar,
And drifts of daffodils delight our eyes.

Thus spring has blossomed forth since time began -
Oh, would that time could hold such hope for man.

Paddy Ariss

AUTUMN

Charcoal trees, devoid of life, gauntly stand
Flirting silver threads woven fine as silken lace.
Clinging in fronds of shimmering pearls glistening raindrops
land
Tearfully upon each skeleton leaf, each blade, each wizened
face.

Fading roses, echoing summer's glory, now are fading,
Shrunken petals, once so proud, weep to see the dying sun.
Silver grasses dewdrop sweet in autumn's shading
Shiver and sigh to the morning chill, now that summer's done.

Gloria Atkinson

WINTER'S SONG

Unseen
A songthrush sings from bare tree-top
On a frosty winter morning
Sun rises through haze icicles drop
As day begins its dawning

Unheard
Along the cliffs above the raging sea
As roaring wind and dragging surf
Pounds beaches mercilessly

Undeterred
The small brown bird sings out her melody
From the sheltered woods the trees resound
With a song much larger than she
The whole valley rings with the solo she sings
Welcoming longer days and the promise of spring.

Christine A Lee

SPRINGTIME

Hark, wait and listen, is that little Jack Horner
Telling us that spring, is just around the corner
The bulbs have started to all peep through
A welcome sight, for me and you.

No more dark mornings or dark nights
No more switching on all the lights
The birds will soon all be singing
And the church bells will be ringing
So hurry up the sun, ,and the nice warm weather
When the dog and I can go out together.

Elizabeth Ann Collis

MARSABIT

Marsabit is a forest oasis, lush as the
desert is dry
Over the parched wilderness, lies a
thick moisture in the sky.

Lake Paradise lies beneath the mist,
where plants and animals do exist
Its rain water makes this desert island blue
On the plants and trees, it leaves a dew.

Cloud and fog forms over the moisture
from the ocean
It cools and condenses as it's in motion
Beneath the volcanic hills lies Lake
Paradise
Staring like an eye at the African sun
Marsabit Island is a mystery, deep in
the heart of the Chalbi Desert.

Rose Bell

APRIL SHOWERS

April showers please fall on me
to wash my eyes that I might see
now wintertime has been and past
and the spring so green is here at last.
A fresh clean smell when clouds have gone
lighter evenings from now on.
So April showers please fall on me
to wash my eyes that I might see
the springtime beauty that at last
has pushed old winter to the past.

Roger Stokes

THE RISING

As spring breaks forth new leaves appear
skies above all blue and clear.
Frosted ground all cracked and bare
new spring coat about to wear.

Tiny heads appear in view
life again all sparkling new.
Pushing forth towards the light
springtime bulbs a welcome sight.

Growing buds on branches bare
shimmering grass so green and fair.
Bursting forth from winter's sleep
rising up from earth so deep.

The singing birds their nests to build
in high tree tops or hedgerow field.
Throbbing, pulsing, a world alive
Mother Nature the power to drive.

Warmth to grow the new life seed
the waiting world the mouths to feed.
Glowing sun the dark depart
life's process a brand new start.

Leon Draper

TO THE SNOWDROP

We sigh for spring, sweet snowdrop shy,
Ring out your glad attire,
And snug beneath your drooping head
The blushing beauty hides.

The winter's sting, its blast has gone
And early spring is nigh,
Sweet snowdrop sad, we are so glad
To see the spring we sigh.

Your quivering bell so sad it hangs
In rich and white array,
To gentle winds in early spring
Your drooping head doth sway.

To gladdening spring the bells do ring,
No more the hoary rime,
Sweet snowdrop sad, sweet snowdrop glad,
For early spring we sigh.

Terrence St John

FOREVER GRATEFUL

Cascading perfumed blossoms
Caressed by gentle breeze
Trees in gowns of pink and white
Delight for all the bees
Cowslips, daises, clover blooming at my feet
Little lambs dance in the grass looking oh so sweet.

Daffodils that look like gold shimmering in the sun
Rabbits running to and fro, having lots of fun
Standing on the rustic bridge, gazing at the stream
Reflects a lovely azure sky, a lovely place to dream.
Down-stream I see a pair of swans such pure and gentle grace
Little cygnets swimming there with beguiling little face.

Everything is now reborn from the dormant state it knew
A world sublime in every way to give us hope anew
Dew glistens just like diamonds in the early sun
Sparkling dewy spider webs where little spiders run
Intoxicating beauty in these precious things I see
I am forever grateful for what God has given me.

Angela Pearson

WELCOME SPRING

Winter's blast has blown away
Chaos from the roads
Spring slips in, decides to stay
With firm blossom, time explodes.

Butterfly from her fairy ring
Escapes an April shower
Stretching throats yearn to sing
Sweet songs from shaded bower.

Nature's growth now free to fill
Winter's path stripped once so bare
Welcome pretty daffodil
Your presence admired everywhere.

Poodle lamb with mother sheep
Instinct, such tender ways.
Watch the weeping willow weep
Overjoyment on spring days.

Waters kiss the hollow'd edge
Free'd from frozen rains
To join the sea a chosen pledge
Meticulously through planet veins.

Welcome spring with all your splendour
May birth and nature all entwine
To taste and scent sweet spring odour
Elated am I to know you're mine.

John Gilbert Conning

COLD MOUNTAINS OF THE NORTH

Winter comes early to the mountains of the north.
With angry blizzards driving forth their dancing snows.
Man will farely dread and rarely tread this place
For there's nothing between here and Siberia.
Only the fear of horizontal blows of frozen needles
In his face, and freezing gales blowing clear
Across ridge and wind-bald peak.

But, the dark valley far below, so grey and bleak
Will know the warmth of the blazing hearth.
For in every stony homestead there's a glowing ingle,
And at the crofter's feet, a galvanised bath full of
Summer-hewn logs, eager to release their summer's heat
And above the moaning sighs of the northerly wind
Are the lonely cries of the shepherd's dogs.

In the still-dark dawn, a dank and cobbled path
Meets the early herdsman. His outline rigid and forlorn
As, in the low doorway he stiffly bows and scrapes
Away uneaten kale. The cows look up from lazy eating
As he pats their boney rumps, Morag, Jane and Abigail,
In familiar greeting.

He drinks from a rusty flask of hot brown tea,
Laced with winter-numbing scotch.
Gathers up his silver pail and, before caressing
Soft warm teats, warms cold hands in corduroy crotch.
And in the cold, cold mountains of the north,
Creamy, steaming milk, sweetly gushes forth.

John Merritt

STORMY SEAS

With the clouds, all leaden grey,
They turn to night, what should be day.
Amidst angry roars, from the mighty seas,
Which flood the shore, relentlessly.
Ebbing and flowing with God like might,
On a winter's day, that's more like night.
The seas with might, rise within this season,
Man knows not why, he cannot reason.
Brought on by wind, wild without a care,
Soon to blow away to who knows where

John J Hudson

THE SUMMER SUN

The winter sun high in the sky won't be with me when I die
The summer sun moving low will shine on me when time to go
No matter when or where I'll be
I need the sun to shine on me.

The flattened grass where I lie
The butterfly flitting by
Sweet songs of birds, the buzz of bees
My head spins with sounds of these.

Darkest corners reached by the sun's warm rays
Light swish of the trees in the gentlest breeze
The rose opens up, its perfume escapes
Wrapped in their shadows, the shrubs take shape.

Breathing in the warm sweet air
There is nothing to compare
With that feeling of being free
Lovely summer stay with me.

Doreen Brooks

SUNSET AND SUNRISE

Glorious sunset
all orange and gold
How you appear
when the day grows
old
like a beautiful rainbow
all shimmering colour
changing palettes
when the day becomes
duller
You fade and die, when
the day becomes night
and the morn brings the
sunrise
all yellow and bright

J Floyd

GIANT'S CAUSEWAY (ULSTER)

Entwined with bracken
And the beckoning waves,
O'erlooked by basalt ocean pipes,
The fierce Atlantic raves
Amidst the polyphonic strains
Of Vulcan's weathered crags
And carved by stormy rains,
Raw nature - the salty tang of sea
And pasture - every living thing
Cries out in exaltation -
Orchestral echoes on the scree.

Nola B Small

CHICKS

These balls of fluff, so small and light,
They make a sweet and delicate sight.

With tiny beaks and dewdrop eyes,
And stalky legs on clutching toes,
Soft chickens chirp and shake,
While mother keeps them safe from foes.

My sister's hands, uncertain, flicker -
Take hold afraid a one-day chick;
Such vices that could snap its twiggy ribs
Or mangle wings like petals
If startled by a stalky flutter.

These bright, shimmering, shivering balls of sun,
Like magnificent tigers, grand yet near extinct,
They shame the work of man.

For what can he create?
A glittering palace of steel and concrete and soot,
Which crumbles, black, to strew the sterile earth with slag.

Self-seeding grass retakes the rubble jigsaw!
The carcass of man's mortal mark,
Once left,
Is dust in nature's wake.

See spring now banish the death of winter,
As leaf-clouds billow from tree-trunk spikes,
Puffed like a yacht's wind-filled sail.

Above, great white clouds cruise on a crystal film,
On the surface of a great waveless ocean.
Beyond, rests the dome of the sky,
Pure blue,
Broken only by the radiant sun.

Paul Butters

THE FALCON FEEDS

Whirling on whispering wings, feathering the still air,
Hovering now, the waiting game, while hungry eyes
Their food to seek, ever alert scan everywhere,
Till swooping swiftly, surely, streamlined sleek, he dives
Another dies.

In vain cacophony of warnings shrill did sound
Eager to satisfy her hungry fledglings small
The thrush, seeking their food tarried late upon the ground
And paid the price, became the hungry falcon's meal,
The fledglings call.

Beaks open wide, blind eyes that cannot see the deed,
Waiting for food that never will arrive,
Helpless without the means to satisfy their needs,
They too will pay the price of swift and vengeful dive.
The falcon feeds.

M Lander

SPRING TIME

When lambs and rabbits jump in the air
New life, full of joy without a care
In the soft green grass they run.
Hares boxing and having fun
Snowdrops with heads hung low
Thrive after the cold winter's snow
Crocus yellow and blue
Cover the ground, a wonderful hue.
Fragrant golden daffodils
Bloom in clusters on the hills
Bluebells blossom in the wood
Fox and squirrel look for food
Nightingale thrush, blackbirds sing
The joy of life in spring.

K Brown

THE WIND

Hear the wind whistling through the trees -
yesterday 'twas but a gentle breeze.
To-day he roars, cannot stay still,
he rushes down valleys, then on up the hill.
Over the roof-tops he speeds on his way
howling along - like a dog at bay.
He catches up leaves, gives them many a whirl,
throws them high in the air, then seems to hurl
them straight down, as he goes on his way,
chortling and laughing, as if to say
'you cannot catch me, try if you can' -
he mocks us all, be we child or man.
We fight hard against him, but are no match -
he rattles the windows, unfastens the latch.
Then just as we're feeling in murderous vein,
he changes his antics, becomes gentle again.
He knows we'll forgive him, when weather turns hot,
and his welcome caresses can help quite a lot -
he tempers the heat, and breathes o'er the land -
in summer he doesn't get out of hand!
We love him then, and this he knows -
but *not* in winter, when he just blows!

Joyce Hockley

AZALEA GARDENS AT MUNCASTER CASTLE

Today I entered paradise
I smelt a fragrance rare
A sweet yet subtle movement
Spoke joy within the air.

Exotic clouds of brilliance
Bright gems amidst the boughs
A sparkling riotous vision
Brushed gently damp my brow.

And was I lost midst dreaming
Of colour, sound and shape?
A scented moist green pathway
Draped o'er with wondrous cape.

Or were my eyes wide open
And was sweet heaven here?
Rich beauty in a garden
Earth's chest of jewels so dear.

Kay Stammers

ORDER OF THE UNIVERSE

Order of the Universe
Planets turning crossing
Co - existing.

Birth death regeneration
The changing seasons
Cycles of creation.

Aspects of the moon
The new the old the dark side
Controlling changing tide.

Perilous craggy
Cliffs drop to the ocean
Wondrous creation.

Vastness continuity
Eternal beauty
Mother Nature

Puts man in perspective -
He thinks *He's* creative!

Rhiannon Phillips

WINTER COME SPRING

Winter is here
How sad it seems
When all that colour
Has gone to seed.

The leaves fall off
Leaving the trees bare
Yet! They still look beautiful
Standing there.

They are all having a rest
You will be pleased to know
And come spring
Out, they will all glow.

I could stand all day
In spring sunshine
Marvelling in 'nature' in everyway.

The cherry trees all of a colour
Yellow forsythia too
All manner of spring shrubs
Intermixed with the evergreens.

We must not forget the lovely
Daffodils, tulips, bluebells and
Our old favourites the forget-me-nots,
Nor the faces of the pansy.

It effects us all does spring
When everything is in bloom.
The splash of colour everywhere
Does everyone the world of good.

Una Gribble

LIFE WITHOUT ANIMALS

Dogs always barking, cats, rabbits
Horses straying, donkeys neighing
Birds with their whistling it's just a habit
Cockerels crowing hens noisily laying
Lambs and sheep frolic and bleat
I don't call this a treat
Insects, fish, crocodiles tiger, hippo
Shoot them all I'd give them jippo
Damn things even frogs are croaking
No need to get alarmed I'm only joking
To be honest have you ever thought
Life would mean nothing, nought.
Without such creatures where would we be?
All the humans for you and me
No insects, for flowers to grow
Potatoes, beans, we could not sow.
The sound of lambs in early spring
Oh what joy it really brings
Cockerels early in the morn
Birds sweetly singing at dawn
Domestic pets, we all agree
Properly handled good to see
Wildlife roaming what a sight
And save them in their plight.

C McCarthy

SUMMER'S A-COMING!

Summer is coming
For spring's now appeared
And daffodils dance in the grass,
I've seen a blackbird and thrush with some straw
For a nest they are hoping will last.

At dawn the light filters
Through windows so small
And birdsong starts early at four
I go back to sleep till I'm wakened at seven
To see light stream bright through the door.

The colours are glorious
Have you tulips pink?
Bright primulae colour the beds
The grass is so green, the beech is in leaf
And the seedlings raise pretty young heads.

I feel happy in winter
Much better in spring,
But when summer is reaching out there
I feel so excited with warmth and bright days
I wish it could stay the whole year.

But then I give thought
What a wonderful gift
God's given, changing seasons each year
For all of us, old, young, infirm or in bed
They bring change and a great deal of cheer.

Elizabeth M Sudder

TREES

As I walk and gaze around
I see the beauty so profound
Of hill dale forest and glen
Of trees made by God for the joy of men
Men who never stop to ponder
The reason there not made for us to plunder.

For I think I shall never see
Any earthly wonder as lovely as a tree
A tree whose hungry roots are spread
Beneath the earth's sweet flowing breast
A tree that looks at heaven all day
To lift her leafy arms to pray.

A tree that in the summer wears
A nest of songbirds in her hair
Upon whose bosom snowflakes have lain
Which introversely lives with rain
Eden's garden not made by fools like me
For only our God can make a tree.

For now my day is ending
Gentle breeze the leaves are bending
Homeward bound my feet are treading
To lay me down on feathered bedding
Eyes to close like the blossom on the tree
My day is done Lord abide with me.

C W Semmens

NATURE

Walking through the countryside
On a bright and sunny day
Can't help noticing
Nature's beauty on the way
Apart from all the plants
And the birds up on the trees
Saw lots of berry bushes
Swarms of wasps and bees
Careful don't disturb them
Or you may feel their wrath
See the little ants
Like an army across our path
Nature really is a joy
An experience not to be missed
When arranging your *day out* agenda
Be sure a country walk's on your list.

Janette Harazny

THE SNOWDROP

A fragile beauty
serenity and stealth,
as winter's hostility takes hold,
breaks through with strength
beyond compare
as buds emerge to winter's cold.
Unfolding,
tender leaves of green,
its crown of white reflects.
The darkest days
the coldest night.
A snowdrop
paves the way.

Michael Cheney

THE WOOD

(Dedicated to Leomansley Wood which is to be desecrated)

The trees stand old and stark.
Gnarled, creaking, and unbespoke.
The branches like arms reach for the sky.
The twigs are fingers perched on high.
They stretch and bend, and clasp.
As if to say I have you now within my grasp.

They whisper, what do they say.
How can you know, how can you tell.
They are not like us, they know too much.
Which means they lack the common touch.

Guardians are they from long long ago
Their secrets they keep, we are not to know.
The wind is not their master, but it makes them bend.
As if to say you have reached the end.
Some will succumb to this power.
The rest will stay for many an hour.

Tread into this wood if you dare.
Remember, remember who might be there.
Be it faun, be it a god, it lurks below the wilted sod.
Desecrate me if you dare.
Attempt to destroy, then see my power.
One thousand years have I been here.
You mortal men I do not fear.

Carl Kemper

CASTING A SHADOW

Blanketing these shores is the darkness of my love.
I am alone amid an awe inspiring beauty.
The warmth of the skies pierces the cutting wind
And welcomes my inner desire.

I cast my shadow, hoping the seeds of my dreams will blush in flower.
My eyes fall upon the thunderous break.
Its eternal anger smashes a rage unrelenting.
This tidal floor, the forever, unforgiving victim.

Awesome cliffs, sheer, silent, haunting, create foreboding.
Time has forged their magnificent, towering strength.
The pulling moon heaves the thrashing tide
Upon fallen rock and beguiling crag.

My naked feet soothed by cool pools of forgotten tide.
The ocean's surf laid out like a white edged cloth
To embellish the shimmering table of shoreline.

I am drowned with unabated passion for this strong
And beautified earth.
Future days will bring my love to these shores
Of Bedruthan.

Mark Jordan

GENTLE PERSUADER

Earth in a mantle of silent snow
Winter's icy breath glides upon the air
Branches, brittle on naked trees
Appear as arms, with hands and fingers bare.
Winter will tighten its icy grip
Before it releases its hold
Until spring, the gentle persuader
Tells the bulbs 'It's the end of the cold.'

Although spring's stay is only brief
It seems a magic spell she weaves
Awakes the earth from a deep cold sleep
And trees will soon unfold new leaves.
Primrose and crocus appearing
Their faces raised to the sun
And once again the birds will sing
To tell us 'Winter's done.'

Betty M Varley

SPRING

When delicate snowdrops
Peep through the snow,
Spring is not far away we know.
Old winter has sprung us many disasters
But we think with joy of what comes afterwards,
Warmer days and lighter nights
And lovely flowers that bring us delights,
Tulips and daffodils nodding their heads,
Seeds seeping through in the vegetable beds.
Forsythia, lilacs and more lovely shrubs,
And lilies will bloom in the patio tubs.
Hurrah for summer to give of its warmth,
And no more fires in the hearth!
Till autumn time comes round again
Full circle and here comes winter time
Again with its pain.
'Tis then I think of spring
And the soft falling rain,
And all the birds do sing again,
And herald again 'tis spring, 'tis spring.

Joan Spain-Smith

THE JOYS OF SPRING

Spring is here once again
Animals watch their young
Kids in the park on the swings
Spring is just such fun
The flowers blossom it looks so nice
The sky so still and blue
The sun is shining above us
There's so much for us to do
Watching the lambs bouncing around
And the bunnies so fluffy and small
It certainly is a perfect picture
I've never seen anything so beautiful at all
The birds are singing in the trees
Singing a merry song
But this will all vanish very soon
'Cos autumn won't be long.

Vicki McIntyre

POETS' DREAM

Ancient hills, steeped history
Thwarted landscape deserted
Fragrant pines veiled by mist
Tapestry woven, nature's mystery.

Tilth, purple mottled jade
Rippling streams peacefully glow
Vermilion sunsets, tinged gold
Horizons distant, water-colours fade.

Enraptured wondrous scene
Timeless grandeur surpassed
Whispering winds, spirit free
Majestic, captivating, poets' dream.

Jean Emerson

THE EMERALD FOREST

Overwhelmed by
Sheer magnificence.
Towering above me are the
Fruits of the forest.
Centuries of existence
Lay before me in a
Wondrous ocean of green.
Forest trails
Canopied by the foliage
Shivers of sunlight reach
The forest floor.
All is calm in this
Brilliance,
Whilst nature struggles
To save another
Emerald forest
From the brutal hands
Of man.

Jennifer Emery

DAFFODILS AND PETUNIAS

Springtime has come
Again thank God
After the long winter's
Frost and cold

The tapestry of colours
Painting nature's canvas
To prepare summer's dawning

People start to smile
Stopping to chat awhile
Spring has come at last
Thank God winter's past

Melfyn Dean

MIDST OF WINTER

Have you been through the woodlands in the snowy
midst of winter
As the brown leaves of autumn are rotting in
the lanes
Have you watched Mother Nature laying down
her pure white carpet.
Down o'er hills and valleys where no two
are the same

Now the songbirds have all left us for to go
to warmer climates
There's just the robins singing in the
pure clean air
Icicles are forming on the outstretched
branches
Of the silent weeping willow and the lively
Christmas fir

Have you watched the snowflakes falling on a
winter's morning
Have you felt them gently melting in your
outstretched hand
And have you seen the snow clouds as they
leave o'er distant mountains
Looking back in silence at the wondrous
virgin land

But now the cold winds have stopped
blowing
The once iced up brook is flowing
And the snow drifts by the hedgerows are
melting in the sun
Wintertime is leaving and springtime is
appearing
One more of nature's seasons has
suddenly begun

Dennis W Dean

SEASONS

In springtime there are
Flowers
In summer fields of gold,
In autumn there are
Yellow leaves,
But winter's bloody cold.

The seasons come so soft
And silent,
Slowly creeping in,
As gently now the tide
It flows
Bringing forth new life,
A life that lasts
But several weeks yet
Never can die out.

With miracles beyond belief
The strangeness of
A lonely heath,
Which silently by winter
Sleeps,
Until the spring has dawned
And beauty springs forth
From its seed
As winter's death is mourned.

So now the time is here
Again
When all shall be revealed,
The smell of sweetest
New mown grass
And summer's golden field.

James Cunningham

THE WORLD ABOUT US

After the wrath, raging winds and snow,
comes the glorious spring, where the orchards gently blow,
After the dark of the night, and daylight peircing through,
Blackbirds shrilly sing out, on the grassy dew,

As the pale sun shines through to brighten up the day,
As squirrels jump out from the willows, and gladly play,
While other birds build their nests, singing with tender voices of ecstasy,
As Mother Nature works hard, for all of us to see,

Daffodils bloom and spring out their yellow faces, and bright heads,
While the contrast colours of the wallflowers of red, orange yellow,
white are seen on their beds,

Crocuses are seen, a beautiful display of blue and white,
As April showers fall down and waters them, such a delight,
To all this loveliness and colouring throughout the spring,
To watch and know that the Lord God Almighty can bring,

To the forget-me-nots, and the bluebells we gather,
While watching strolling, and viewing together,
The beautiful different shades of tulips will bloom out, and contented
in the sun,
While Mother Nature still works hard, until the day is done,

Apple blossom, lilac, may, and to the chestnut trees,
Spreading their leaves whispering to the warmth of the sunshine and
gentle breeze,
These lovely trees that seem to look up proudly all day,
Until we come into glorious May,

The nightingale will soon bring out his notes of cheer,
Watching his mate as she hatches her grey green eggs, while he sits near,
The lovely sounds of sweet, tac, as now they both sing out their notes,
Showing their white breasts across their throats,
Underneath the wonderous moon, as it brightens the dark sky.

All this lovely nature free, not even money can buy,
From God's own work who made everything to the various flowers
that blossom in April and May
From those wintry, raging winds that disappeared and quickly blew away,

Jean McGovern

I LET MY CAT OUT AND . . .

Tree dandruff,
Petal snow;
Oh wishing well wonder,
Oh

This Garden of Eden

Falls so serene,
Blessing fresh grass
And all in-between.

Under a beautiful haze of perfumed streets
I pause to inhale my memories of summer,
Wave to the milk bottles rattling in darkness,
My bare legs flattered by early warmth.

Decorate this picture
With pink beetle hats
And dew ant shelter.

Tree dandruff,
Petal snow;
Little houses of nature
Shine through my closing door . . .

Ernest Ravenstoic

FIRST SEASON

Did I hear the bluebells ring,
To say at last it is spring?
The daffodils nod their heads.
Stand proudly in flower beds.
The blackbird sings with delight
His song heard from morn 'til night.
Skylarks' songs heard way on high
Looking down from a blue sky.
Ploughmen keep straight and narrow.
Make sure of an even furrow.
Seed that's scattered all around.
Soon sprouts from a fertile ground.
Raincoats, brollies are put away,
Children laugh, there's games to play
Church bells ring, the bride looks fine.
Soon is saying, 'I'll be thine,'
Cast those winter blues aside,
With a smile your troubles hide,
Life's not full of woe and dread,
Happiness is yours to spread.

Jim Dolbear

UNTITLED

Builders encroach on the countryside,
Some part disappears every year.
Fields taken over for new roads,
To cater for lorry or car.

Will the world be a concrete jungle
Is the fear of so many of us.
But I can see a glimmer of light,
When I travel on foot or by bus,

For wherever a building's demolished,
Bricks and stones left to litter the ground;
Grasses and flowers push their way through,
Wherever a crack can be found.

For nature is not easily beaten,
She'll flourish whenever she can,
And still carry on when buildings are dust,
And maybe survive even man.

Lucy Alltoft

LOVE OF SPRING

Golden glowing trumpets
Blowing gently in the wind,
Oh, how I love the daffodils
Bright heralders of spring

Fluffy white clouds drifting
Across a pale blue sky,
Stately trees their green coats don
To please the artist's eye.

The crocus and the hyacinth
Push their heads up through the earth
The sounds of morning birdsong
Oh! Sweet season of rebirth

Lambs gambolling in verdant grass
The winds of March that bring
April's refreshing raindrops
Rejoice once more it's spring.

When all around us life returns
After its long deep sleep
To let us know continuity
Of time is ours to keep.

Kathleen Finney

DAFFODIL VALLEY

Sunshine and early spring,
The earth awakes
And sheds her wintry garb,
Relaxes in the warmth,
And brings forth pristine buds
Of violet, almond pink
And golden yellow

The country calls again,
And urges us to speed
Over the dipping Wolds,
Until we catch our breath
And gaze from Surprise View
Into the hidden valley,
Whose green banks rise
From the trickling stream,
And like yellow daubs of paint
The clustered daffodils
Are splashed against the green.

What perfect flowers these wild ones are,
Their trumpets bravely raised
Against the sharpened winds
That blow across the dale
From hill and moor -
Brave harbingers of Yorkshire's spring
They live from far and wide
The tourist, rambler, passing motorist,
Who dons his boots to tread the muddy path
Along the golden route
Of Daffodil Valley.

Margaret Turtle

WE MAKE A HAPPY PAIR

Spring is in the air
with the trees in glorious blossoms
of pinks and whites
with daffodils and tulips
what a wonderful sight.
We walk hand in hand
along the path through the meadow
of buttercups and daisies,
it's like the promised land
especially now the days are longer
and we have more sunlight.
Love is in the air
with the perfume of the roses
we make a happy pair.
The ducks and swans have their mate
and on the moonlit lake they swim.
I am so lucky as I have you to date
a love like ours is so special and rare.
Kiss me and hold me,
for you I really care.
This feeling is rather wonderful.
Isn't it great.
Isn't it grand,
when romance is in the air.

Rosemary Medland

GARDENS

Gardens around us full of colour just now
Gnomes on the lawns taking a bow
Red and yellow tulips in full bloom
Lifting the wintry gloom
Easter daisies in flower they were late
Now they're blooming it was worth the wait
Cherry trees around with blossom so pink
A pleasure to look at that's what I think
Worms and insects the birds are seeking
Young ones in their nests are peeking
Watch out for the cat it's on the prowl
Now the dog begins to growl
Nature around for all to see
Now what's that I see
It's a buzzy busy bee.

B W Jones

A PRELUDE TO SPRING

If the sun would only shine,
I could hang my clothes on the line,
See the freshness shake about,
And in the disappearing snow,
They in spring's awake,
Bring yellow, clean faced daffodils,
In clusters around my garden gate,
As cobwebs from each corner sweep,
Spring-cleaned from winter's sleep,
There sunshine tells, picks up the light,
That sparkles upon trinkets on the shelves,
Across the threshold inside the home,
On mother's day the cards and gifts behold,
Making a heart to sing, in loved ones' arms to cling,
So lovely is this prelude to spring.

Joan McAvoy

THE GLORIOUS SUN

Clear blue heaven on a sunlit day,
Lovers laying in a field of hay,
Oh what a beautiful summer's morn,
Feeling happy I was born.
Tractor rolling down the lane,
Clear days forecast, no more rain,
Oh and I'm happy, oh so glad,
After the winter we just had.

Children making daisy chains,
Field mice scurry eating grains,
Oh and I smile when I see,
My lover's eyes shine at me.
A butterfly settles on a thorny rose,
We settle down nose to nose,
Appreciating the summer's charms,
We lay together in each other's arms.

Feeling so pleasant the sunny rays,
Minds drift off on a shimmering haze,
Brought back swiftly with the call of a bird,
That since last summer has not been heard.
Far away across the county line,
A single dog tells the world he's fine,
Although he's not the only one,
Brought to life by the glorious sun!

Mark Ringsted

JUST ANOTHER LAMB (CONSEQUENCES)

Just another lamb, of hundreds new-born,
This one perhaps an hour old.
Unsteady legs, tottering, already forlorn
Ten feet away its mother is chewing
The new lamb is struggling.

Just another lamb, there are dozens in view,
This one perhaps three hours old.
Moving uncertainly, uneasily from ewe to ewe
Frightened, bleating, are you my mother it seems to be asking.
Twenty feet away its real mother is chewing.

Just another lamb, on this thirteenth day of May,
This one confused, disoriented, perhaps five hours old.
Now as the evening draws in, becoming cold,
The lamb starts to run a little but not in fun
Or exploration; more in panic and desperation
And follows another ewe from one side of the field
To the other and back again.
The real mother is nowhere to be seen.

Just another lamb, so many others sleeping
And snuggling up to their mums,
This one born perhaps twelve hours ago.
Unsuckled, unwanted, now lies dead.
In the middle of the field a small bloody bundle.
Yesterday such a small life,
Now a carrion crow's breakfast
The new day hardly begun.
Today many more will be born;
Gladly most will survive
As nature takes its course
With neither rewards nor punishments
Just consequences.

John Gordon

THE COMMON

The breezes are balmy, the sunshine is bright
The blackthorns are covered in billowy white
Where the common lay dead there are violets pale blue
Primroses, celandines, dandelions too

The distant hills beckon through shimmering haze
But we just prefer on the common to laze
The dogs lie panting in the green willow's shade
In summer we bask in this cool woodland glade

We traverse the common in old faded suit
To harvest the blackthorn's frosted blue fruit
Late autumn they ripen to make fine red wine
For Christmas good cheer when we sit down to dine

We're tramping around the old common again
It's cold, bleak and windy and threatening rain
The trees and the bushes their leaves have now shed
Warm days, like the swallows, have far away fled

Brown is the bracken, lying flat on the ground
Forlorn seem the blackthorns sleeping around
No birds here to cheer us with their trilling song
Just the moan of the river tumbling along

Today it is colder and what do you know
The common is covered with sunshine and snow
Children just love it and find it a thrill
To build a huge snowball to roll down the hill

Again the scene changes and now with a roar
The wind and the rain sweep the common once more
Spring may be nigh but sadly we say
We're not going out on the common today

Reg Harper

THE GREENMAN

He stands there, tall and majestic,
In his livery of green and brown.
With his head, held high in the clouds;
His feet, firmly planted in the ground.
With the burdens of life on his shoulders,
From which there'll be no rest,
And the love for all things natural,
Burns fiercely in his breast.

He's the essence of the seasons,
He brings rain, sun and snow.
From him the druids gained wisdom;
Which enabled mankind to grow.
Endowed with mystical authority,
From conception, through to birth.
And for time eternal he will be,
The sentinel for Mother Earth.

His name, has long been forgotten,
And the Celtic gods are no more.
But his wonders are still around us,
In the skies and valley floors.
His home is in the greenwoods,
His body, the mighty oak tree.
And the spirit of the greenman,
Still lives on in you and me.

We are the greenman's children,
Like the flowers, birds and trees.
We are of the highest order,
In his plans of creativity.
So no more shall we plunder nature;
Taking, without any return.
But re-establishing the natural balance,
Should be mankind's main concern.

W Tony Crowther

THE GREAT CUILLIN OF SKYE

In days before time
Giants fell from your shattered summits
Scratching and tearing in desperation
Crashing down to dark and secret corries.
So, the desolate nugget of Cuillin was born.

Silent and sulking in the groin of the world
Pregnant with power and primordial lust.
Awesome rock spewed from the bowels of earth
Violently vomited from the raging furnace.
Heart of earth manifest and visible,
The essence of life is brooding in your high places
Where my restless spirit longs to dwell.

A friend out in the madness,
Away from the fast and frivolous virtual reality
That has no place in the glory of nature.
Mankind lies imprisoned in its concrete cage
Chasing the wind.

Oh, mighty Cuillin, the heart of unknowing,
How I long to be lost on your thundered peaks
Where the shattered rock spits water into cascading burns
Swelling the turgid tumescence of hungry lochs,
Transfusing the surging and pulsing creative force.

Oh, antlered matador of the spindrift cape
Dog-toothed and broken Goliath of Skye,
Magnificent mountain of my waking dream
You re-kindle my passion for life.
Lead me from darkness to crystal day
Your deep velvet shadows are conduits of hope and release.
Eternal companion and keeper of souls.

Chris Thomas

THE PRESENT MOMENT

Time like a rapid stream
flows swiftly by
we have but a moment
as it passes through

Each moment that we are
is gone never to return
the future never comes
then is gone forever

Only the present moment
is our possession of time
while we look to the future
it is gone unheeded

Were they well spent
or did they drift away
those precious moments
which compose our day

Our future dreams
are yesterday
and we have lost
ourselves and our today.

B J Bramwell

MY GARDEN OF DREAM

If I were a gardener, in the land of nod,
A beautiful stream running through my plot!

Forget the peas and carrot, or the bean and spud,
Shrubs, flowers and roses should grace the land of mine!

Trees mixed with lilacs for the spring,
For birds to nest and sing!

Then amongst the roses and by the tree,
A secluded seat to rest for me!

Dreaming, in the shade on hot summer's days,
Until late last night, listening with delight.

To the bird's song, and the gurgling stream,
That will be my guitar, the music to my ear,
Happy and serene, in this garden of my dream.

Anna Elliott

LOOK AROUND

I often sit and think about, what our lives would be like
Without the trees and flowers, or an animal in sight
What a dull old place this world would be
Without the grass, the hills the sea.
With no birds singing, come each dawn
No summer sun to keep us warm.
No farmers ploughing up the furrows
No rabbits hopping to their burrows
No new born lambs so gaily playing
No sound of that old donkey braying
No flowers blowing in the breeze
Nor leaves that flutter from the trees.
So cherish them all whilst we still can
Before they're destroyed by modern man
So that future generations can see
The world the way it was meant to be
Each and all should have a duty
To contribute to nature's beauty
For what a sad old world this place would be
Without these things for us to see.

Dorothy Cirillo

WHEAT HILL

Snowdrops are our welcome, uniting us with spring.
Leaping from damp, mossy roots, in gentle breeze they swing.
Swirling as the ripples, over once a dormant lake,
As they venture up the hillside, where in clusters,
Congregate.

Cherished are their petals, as in crowds they sway in time,
Sweetly, they sing in whisper, when their dainty stems
Combine.
Dancing to the chorus, clothed in silken costume white,
Expressing spring's arrival, with a dazzling message bright.

Annually, they take their path, Wheat Hill their destiny,
Awakening the undergrowth and calling to the tree.
Stirring as the joyful hare, leaps in bounds of play,
Picturesque they shine in morning's sun; a perfect spring
Bouquet.

Sara Russell

FULL SUMMER

Colour of marigold
    held in the sky.
Green of trees
    full in their leaves.
Ripples of water
    dappled in shade.
Summers in plenty
    with the ripening of land.
Drowsy of bee
    heavy with pollen.
Cry of the swallow
    in love with the air
Life at its fullness
    no more shall I need.

Sandra E Kirton

NATURE'S BOOK

Wandering along hand in hand, at peace
with heaven and earth.
The sun is warm, the sky is blue,
dazzling with its hue.

The trees all around are budding, hear the babbling
of a brook,
So many beautiful things to see, in nature's
picture book.

Walking on the river bank, into a pleasant glade,
Bursting with daffodils, in every
sunshine shade.

Sitting on a fallen tree, birds darting
here and there,
The tinkling of a waterfall, carried on
the air.

The hills so high, on every side, majestic in
their stance.
There goes a busy honey bee, doing a merry
dance.

All these beautiful sights and sounds,
Are there if you really care,
But! The most wonderful thing of all,
It's there for us all to share!

Blanche Middleton

NATURE KNOWS NO BOUNDARIES

The winter snows, defrosted now
but chills, still in the air.
A tiny snowdrop pokes up its head
as if it doesn't care.

It warms my heart, it cheers me
and makes me want to smile.
This tiny thing still survives
it just looks *too* fragile.

But, nature knows no boundaries
her blooms she will not delay.
In spite indifferent weather
she puts on her finest display.

Observe her, look around you
all life new, springing forth.
It's something so very wonderful
be it south, west, east or north.

Renewing life not once, nor twice
Nature works the seasons round.
The only thing she does require
is to be left to her own ground.

And when all rebirth is over
She carefully dies things to rest,
then waits again 'til time is right
and once more she'll do her best.

Pam Bateson

THE WONDER OF NATURE

Nature is a wondrous thing
From spring in to the fall
No matter what you may have seen
Surprises are in store
In springtime come the sweetest lambs
To charm us with their grace
Soon birds will wake us with their song
When dawn brings each new day
In summer comes the magic
Of the smaller streams and pools
Where tadpoles, newts hatch out from spawn
And stay there where it's cool
When trees shed leaves in autumn
The squirrels gather nuts
Then store them till it's winter
When food gets very sparse
In winter with the colder days
The dormouse, hedgehogs sleep
They hibernate where there is warmth
For winter can be bleak
And strange enough when seasons change
From winter into spring
We gaze once more with wonderment
At all that nature brings

Jeanette Gaffney

SEASONS OF THIS WORLD

The trees are bent but not broken by the
hostility of the wind.
Nature seems to hide, sky being empty, no
flowers.
They have kept their contract not wishing to
rescind
but I ask where are these awesome powers?

At last one begins to see a hint of sunlight
although there is still far too much rain.
The lambs still spring forth looking - oh
so bright.
While other creatures soon forget the winter's
strain.

Nice hot days start to flow freely for the
flowers to reach their full.
Cats lounge about lapping it up and bees
buzz, singing a song.
You would think that this world could never
look dull
but we know that the natural way may not last for
long.

Crunch, the leaves are now on the ground.
The field mouse is lost, consumed by his dreams
and grain is being stored in barns, huge and round.
How peaceful this world *seems!*

Donna Baxter

HARVEST TIME

Rejoice as we celebrate harvest's rich yield,
The produce of garden and orchard and field:
The promise fulfilled that, while earth shall prevail,
Our sowing and reaping shall never more fail,
Both staples of diet (potatoes and wheat)
And luxury fruits we enjoy for a treat.
Through frost, hail and snow, and through sunshine and rain,
The fullness of harvest is with us again.

Rejoice for the harvest we almost forgot:
Young tender green peas eaten straight from the pod,
First early potatoes so round and so white,
And crisp baby carrots that crunch as we bite,
Plump strawberries picked but an hour ago,
And redcurrants glistening like rubies aglow.
Not only in autumn does harvest abound:
In each passing season earth's riches are found.

Rejoice for the harvest that nobody sees:
The flowers' sweet nectar that strengthens the bees,
Lush grass in the pasture where cattle can feed,
A clump of dank nettles where butterflies breed,
Bright berries that blackbirds devour with zest,
And old rotting logs which the woodlice love best,
The young shoots of heather that nourish the grouse,
Dry grass seeds collected by shy harvest mouse.

Thus is nature's bounty
Lavished far and wide,
That all God's creatures, small and great,
May know their wants supplied.

Margaret Corker

WHY IS IT?

Why is it that as one chapter begins another one closes?

Why is it that as seasons change, our lives do to?

Only the seasons change in circles of months, lives change in circles of years.

Why is it, that we remember our infant years with warm and sunny affection
and our latter years as being cold and critical?

The years in-between are remembered as being tentative, and experimental.

And then in our twilight years, with maturity do we learn to appreciate so
much, that was too easily dismissed when young?

Things that came by so easily, things that could have been changed,
decisions reversed, things that were taken for granted.

You don't heed warnings when time is plentiful, and unlimited, you just
become complacent.

It's only when the years creep up on you, like the changing seasons, the chill
of a September morning, the creaking of an ageing bone.

Why is it then that, we pull on extra layers for warmth and comfort,
or migrate to warmer climates?

Why is it Mother Nature never imparts her eternal secrets, how is it possible
to grow old gracefully, when our bodies become wizened, worn out,
and racked with pain?

Why is it some people retain youthful beauty, or others have the capacity
for storing knowledge?

Why does time have to capture our lives, drawing over us a foggy veil,
making some live out their final years in damp despair?

So why is it, that when life discontinues, the seasons don't,

Why is it?

We don't have all the answers.

T Newton

THE WONDERS OF SPRING

Everywhere the signs of spring,
The birds in full voice, do sing,
In the garden, they chase around,
Until a new partner, they have found,
Mating season, it's plain to see,
She says to him 'Come and catch me,'
The trees have started to go green,
The buds appearing, can be seen,
The bulbs all showing their colourful heads,
As they sit there, in the flower beds,
The daffodils stand tall with pride,
They pop their buds, no longer hide,
No longer short, the grass does grow,
It's quite long, will have to mow,
The sun is warm, the sky so bright,
Insects and bugs, are now in sight,
A butterfly so elegant and free,
Flew over my head, the first to see,
The young are born, in the fields are seen,
The signs of these, spring is what it means,
My dog, he tends to be a pain,
He's losing his winter coat again,
His fur he leaves, everywhere,
Another sign, that spring is there,
This is the best time of the year,
Life so new, it does appear,
Plants and insects and animals,
The wonders of spring, shown to us all.

Lynn Hallifax

THE CHANGING SEASONS

Spring is here and Mother Nature takes
Her magic wand and quietly wakes, the sleeping tree and flower,
the oak and daffodils are stirred,
and in the distance can be heard,
the cuckoo call from Mother Nature's bower.

Tread softly for beneath your feet,
the bluebells and the violets sweet, carpet the fragrant woods with blue,
and new born lambs so soft and white,
gambol in the fields in sheer delight,
and life begins again - anew.

Summer is here and Mother Nature takes,
Her magic wand and gaily makes, a wonderland of beauty to behold,
the foxgloves in profusion grows,
and softly scented silken rose,
exquisitely hued red, pink and gold.

Weep on oh weeping willow tree,
Summer's short lived as we shall see, and southward soon the birds will fly,
now ripened fruit falls to the earth,
silent is Mother Nature's mirth,
as the flowers fade and die.

Autumn has come and Mother Nature takes,
Her magic wand and sadly breaks, summer's blithe, enthralling spell,
so leaves turn yellow, red and brown,
and gusty winds then blow them down,
as lonely, bitter tears from heaven fell.

So winter reigns and Mother Nature takes,
her magic wand and gently flakes, the cold bleak land with snow,
is Mother Nature softly crying?
Or is it just the north wind sighing,
for the sleeping world below.

Pamela Eckhardt

SUNPOWER

Light, pour from me,
ooze from me,
let me burst out,
in the universal
night.
Let me burn with high
passion,
in white nuclear
fashion,
bringing you joy,
and giving you
life.

Rachel Oxtoby

DAFFODILS

With their nodding yellow heads,
They greet the coming spring,
They trumpet 'Welcome' to the birds
And all the songs they sing.

They sway with pleasure in the breeze,
And shine just like the sun,
They spread their warm and yellow glow
Until the day is done.

They brighten up the hills and vales,
And even window sills,
So beautiful, and oh so Welsh,
The yellow daffodils.

Jayne Jenkins

MOTHERING SUNDAY 1996
VIV AND ME

On Mothering Sunday such a sunny day
Decided on a picnic and soon we were on our way
Went to Snowdrop Valley, found a lovely spot
Ken got his stove, had a cuppa nice and hot
Looked at the scenery, it was a lovely view
It really took your breath away, between me and you
Just a white blanket, spread out everywhere
It was so relaxing, in all that fresh air
After our picnic, and a cup of tea.
We went for a walk, did our Viv and me.
As we walked along, someone followed us around.
We saw him taking pictures of the white blanket ground.
Hello, you two young ladies, can I bother you please
Can I take your pictures, will you just say cheese.
I'm with the ITV, taking pictures of Devon
To have your lovely faces on, that would be just heaven.
So look for us in future, when we are on TV
Then tell all your friends, you know Viv and me
We will sign our autographs, of that we have no doubt
And being as you are a friend, we will charge you nowt.

Joan Jeffries

SCOTLAND

Walking in the countryside on a bright summer's day
fields glistening from the sun's golden ray.
Looking across the meadow is a wondrous sight
buttercups and daisies, a mass of yellow and white.

Strolling through the glen, up over the brae, air filled with
the scent of a warm summer's day.
Butterflies flutter, almost floating in the breeze,
crickets chirp in the grass, birds sing in the trees.

Down through the valley, the valley so green
the river flowing in a gentle stream.
Drooping branches from the willow bobbing to and fro
caught in the river's gentle flow.

As the sun begins to set and dusk draws near
I must leave this place that I hold so dear.
Now I set off home passing fields of corn
oh how I love this beautiful land, this land where I was born.

Joan Graham

MEMORIES

Often when I'm all alone
And seated in my chair
My mind goes back to holidays
And happy days spent there.
I'm back in bonny Scotland
Among the glens and lochs
With glorious hills around me
And heather covered rocks.
I travel on to lakeland
Ever fresh and green
My heart is filled with longing
For all that I have seen.
I see the valleys once again
The mountains too of Wales
I've visions too of moorlands
And the lovely Yorkshire dales.
Even when the skies are grey
And winter snows are here
I can wander where I will
With memories so dear.

Barbara J Page

AUTUMN TIME

An early morning mist
Caresses the outstretched fields
Cows herding by the gate
Waiting to give their yield

The dampness of the morning
Clings to bushes and the trees
Flowers breathe their last breath
Now the summer has had to leave

Leaves turning sienna brown
Fall softly to the floor
The wind gathers them together
As the rain begins to pour

Migrating birds glide quietly by
On the way to a foreign land
To enjoy African sunshine
Now that autumn has fallen on our land

A heavy frost outlines the shapes
Eyes do not normally see
Sunlight bounces off frozen pond
A sight given to us for free

Dark mornings, shadows in the evening
A chill that grips the spine
It was a distinctive beauty
This season, autumn time

Stephen Wain

OUR LAKE DISTRICT

Kendal gone past, the mountains in view,
Windermere hides in the trees.
'Let's cross by ferry, the car can come too'
We reach little Hawkeshead with ease.

A short drive to Coniston, steamer to sail,
Climb the *Old Man* before tea.
Go out for a drink, spend the night over here,
Tomorrow there's so much to see.

Tilberthwaite Gill and Wetherlam climbed
Back down over Slaters Bridge.
Up Wrynose Pass over Crinkle Crags
Exhausted we traverse the ridge.

Langdale is slept in and Grasmere next.
We sing out in Rydal Cave.
Dove Cottage is viewed, the *Lion & Lamb* done,
Hellvellyn? Are we feeling that brave?

To Keswick to shop and down to Derwent
Onto Honister Pass and Haystacks.
Great Gable can wait along with Sca Fell
We need a rest for our poor aching backs.

Drive past Crummock Water to Whinlatter Pass,
Cup of tea before Bassenthwaite.
Skiddaw smiles at us but we climbed that last time.
We get round to Ullswater late.

A boat trip is taken, the lake is explored,
Picnic lunch up by Aira Force.
It's time to go home. Lanty Tarn? There's no time?
'Shall we be back?' 'Oh yes! Of course!'

C Bullivent

THE START OF SPRING

The sun shone bright at nine today,
And her warmth was felt by all.

In mid afternoon a light breeze
got up to bring in a little chill.

Magpies drinking from the pool,
and collecting food.

Carp swimming around the pond,
Feeding as they go.

Curlews fill the field by the dykes,
where the land is very wet,
In their hundreds they do feed
and then fly away.

A pair of magpies climb up the silver birch,
Observing comings and goings of other birds.
From birch tree to television aerial they pass
to their second observation post.

Newborn lambs with their mums
moving along the grassy slope
running down to the river crouch.

Daffodils growing in grass verges by the road,
showing off their brightest gold.

Crocus gold, white and purple
growing in clumps glistening in the sun.

G F Snook

LOVE'S HARVEST

Love spins a cloak of sunbeams to warm dear Mother Earth
Pours love sweet wine of April, rejoicing spring's rebirth.
The dear Lord shows His children, the ways of His great love.
Now let Him reap our praises, from His great throne above.

Love dwells within strong branches that bear sweet tempting fruits.
Dear love brings forth the glory, that hides in tender shoots.
The dear Lord shows His children, how great true love can be.
Now let us sing His praises, in great voice joyfully.

Love tints, those rainbow flowers, that 'tice each honey-bee.
To store their precious nectar, in hives for you and me
The dear Lord shows His children, the truth of His great love.
Now let Him reap our praises, from His great throne above.

Love rides the summer breezes, that turn green seeds to gold.
So man can store their beauty, before bleak winter's cold.
The dear Lord shows His children, how great true love can be
Now let us sing His praises, in great voice joyfully.

Love breeds the many creatures, that live beneath the sea.
Grows love the food for cattle, that graze contentedly,
The dear Lord shows His children, the light of His great love.
Now let Him reap our praises, from His great throne above.

Yes, let Him reap our praises.
Our thanks, our joy, our love.

Violet M Corlett

THE ENCHANTED WOOD

This ancient wood has seen a thousand years
Of thrusting growth, proud prime and slow decay,
When fallen trees decline, the sapling gains,
Though trees may die, yet still the wood remains.
Nature and time have spun a magic web
Upon the looms of winter branches bare,
And every season weaves in new delights
Of winter dawns, or singing summer nights.
Before the spring has clothed the trees with leaf,
The rooks their twiggy homes begin to build,
Raucous and comic, black as any bat,
They fill the wood with their domestic chat.
Birdsong enchants the fragile days of spring,
When snowdrops quiver at the feet of trees,
Ghostly they gleam, all night, like moonlight spilled
In woodland hollows autumn leaves have filled.
Summer works magic with a haze of green
Of every shade, from beech's tender leaf
To snake green ivy, climbing to the light
On some great forest stalwart, battening on its might.
The fogs of winter liberate the trees,
Unrooted and ethereal they float,
And last, the whirling flakes on north winds blow
The ultimate magic - woodlands in the snow.

Patricia Taylor

MAIDEN SPRINGS

Spring breezes in with her smiling face,
Pushing hard cold winter out of place.
He once mighty, strong and so bold,
With firm, icy fingers, to keep his hold.
Now passive, whispering spring mild and sweet,
Nimbly climbs aboard her seasonal seat.
She observes the land she's had to prepare,
With a cool contented, hazy-eyed stare.
She appeared in winter from time to time,
Angering winter with her welcome shine,
Busy, she'd only prepared work to be done,
Needing help from her warm, awakening sun.
Spring now lovingly nurtures her fruits,
Encouraging growth from buds and shoots.
Under Mother Nature's beady, critical eyes,
Springtime weeps, laughs and gentle sighs.
Her strong emotions move everything,
To want to expose itself to virgin spring.
The height of her work comes oh, too soon
Spring admires her handiwork in glorious bloom.
Slowly colours and petals begin to fade away,
Exhausted, weary spring knows she's had her day.
Bright, brassy summer marches through the door,
Leaving spring to sleep, tired and footsore.

Jackie Statham

NATURE

Nature is all around us
The animals in the fields,
flowers and the trees
when we go for a walk
we can feel a breeze

My favourite is the snow-drop
They pop their little heads up
Then we know that winter
is over and soon the time will
come for holidays sand, sea and sun.

Every year it is the same the
sun, wind rain and snow
Spring, summer, autumn, winter
The seasons come and go.

J Pearson

WHAT A WONDERFUL WORLD

As the trees grow back their leaves
And also the sound of the humming bees
With corn in the field and the sugar-beet too
The farmer and his men know just what to do
Birds chirping a merry sound
As animals come out to laze around
With the sweet smell of perfume
As the flowers come into full bloom
Children playing out in the sun
Only means that spring has come
Just look around and the pleasure it will give
Shows what a wonderful world in which we live.

Trish Chandler

CAGED

What is it like to be free?
Freedom to me is only a memory.
When will I be able to sleep under the stars?
Without the boundaries of these bars?
Confined to a cage, kept under lock and key,
What is it like to be free?
There is no way that I can describe my anger and despair,
I've tried to explain, but does anybody care?
Does anyone understand how I feel, does anyone see?
What is it like to be free?
No room to move about,
Human kindness I'm beginning to doubt.
Wondering if I was better off being shot at with a gun,
At least then I had somewhere to run.
Inside my mind I am crying,
But inside my heart I am dying.
Staying alive is just prolonging my agony,
What is it like to be free?

Dawn Rumsey

THE RIVER

Weeping willows wash the bank
light dances on the water's surface
shimmering, shining reflection
A flutter of feathers
a flash of wing
The swan makes a spectacular landing
Others join in haste
eager for the taste, of bread
Boats drift idly by
The only sounds,
the gentle lapping of water
And a child's excited cry.

Nicola Grant

SPRING CLEANING

Nature spring cleans with her April showers,
Washing the dust away,
Blowing dead leaves, tidying up,
Brightening the sullen days,
Then polishing sun and stoking the fire,
Providing the warmth for us all,
Stretching the daylight, to fit the frame,
Exciting, delighting us all,
Conducting the chorus of newly born lambs,
Choreographing dances of hares,
Painting the landscape vivid and strong,
Sculpting the circles and squares,
Mending the ravages of seasons past,
Drying the spongy ground,
Arranging the blossom, waking the blooms,
Refreshing, with dew all around,
Inflaming the evening, by knighting the day,
Heralding dawns inception,
Bringing up spring, who is warmly received,
Unlike winter's frosty reception.

Thomas A Rattray

NATURE'S BLANKET

Softly falls the snow,
The flakes fall gently to the ground
Silently, silently not a sound
Warmly covering all around

A fluffy white blanket now covers the earth
The little bulbs and seedlings snuggle down deep,
The snow will cover and protect them
During their winter sleep.

Safe and secure until springtime comes
Nature's duvet will nurture and keep them warm
While enveloped under this gentle blanket
They will come to no harm.

There they will stay until spring comes again
Spurred on to growth by sun and gentle rain
A myriad of colour and beauty on show
Hidden all winter by the covering of snow.

Elizabeth Amery

RAINSTORM

The sky grows dark as the black clouds approach
Causing premature nightfall to quickly encroach
The wind begins to strengthen, the trees move to and fro
As if wanting to run but knowing not where to go

Once the rain begins it's as though it will never stop
Falling as a torrent, not drop by drop
Within minutes it has soaked everything in sight
Pounding the ground with all its might

So hard does it rain the noise it is so loud
Like continuous rolling thunder with a distant cloud
The gutters overflow they simply have no hope
The roads are like rivers as the drains they cannot cope

The world outside becomes like a frosted blur
As like a solid sheet of water the rain it does occur
But at last what seemed forever is beginning to relent
The fury of the storm has been well and truly spent

The black clouds move on, the wind begins to ease
What nature did with such ferocity can also appease
Blue sky breaking through, the trees stand still and tall
Before very long it will be as if it never happened at all.

W Lister

WHEN HEAVEN SHOUTS

Echoing rumbles,
From dark lofty chambers,
Heaven's eyes flash in protest,
Pent up passions of the skies
Explode in anger when heaven shouts.

Its deafening presence descends
And earth trembles in its wake,
Hardly daring to look
The storm in the eye.
She bears the tumult of the skies,
Mistress of the raging monster.

Echoes fade when the shouting's done,
Still tense earth holds her breath,
Her natural rhythm not yet restored.

At last, in final manic throes
The sky pours out its heart,
Anger and passion spent,
Floods the earth with sorrow,
Repenting its vehement wrath.

Cascading rivers shrink to gentle drops,
The crisis has passed.
Earth soaks up heaven's tears,
Heaven is forgiven.

Mary Care

SPRING

Spring is here and flowers bloom
Their fragrance seems to fill the room
Birds sing and are at their best
As they fly and build their nest

The sun is warmer and grass is green
As winter departs you see where it's been
The trees were bare all around
The hardness that was in the ground

The sparrows and starlings here and there
looking to build their nest somewhere
They flutter here to pick up sticks
To make a home for their new chicks

The apple blossom and the privet hedge
All send their blossoms to force a wedge
Into the grip of winter's cold
Whose force doesn't seem to be so bold

I am so glad that summer's near
And summer clothes I now can wear
And take a walk down blooming lanes
The springtime grip has started to gain

The birds do sing and play about
And I can dance and start to shout
Winter has gone it's no longer dark
I can walk and sit in the park

Harriet Wright

NATURAL ELEMENTS

Afraid, yet in awe of erupting volcano,
scarlet flowing larva stream, oh
what a sight to see;
forest fires, raging inferno, flee
to safety in babbling stream,
rain falling on the heat, steam.
A few Rain Forests still survive,
providing protection for creatures to thrive.
Rushing and splashing of waterfall,
still quicksand, waiting to maul!
Waves, rolling, foaming, breaking,
on many land's beaches, baking
deserts of scorching hot sand,
where frozen icebergs would be in demand.
Around and above us, oxygen, invisible air,
essential to life, combustion fire.
Atmosphere, mixture of gasses surrounding Earth,
is the hole in the Ozone caused by pollution's birth?
Horror at destruction Earthquakes and tornadoes can do,
Nature is unpredictable at times, like an element stew!
We humans have learned to harness
the elements provided, to work for us;
But nature's resources are not endless,
do we still have time for, redress?

Anita Fellowes

PEEK! PEAK! PIQUE

Snowy salients
Twin track
Tower peripheral
Hemming
Concave quilted fertile fields
Dreaming down
Vanishing valleys,

Flying fast
Foetal fashion
Chair chained
Wire umbilical
Breach birthed
Feet first
Snow waddling
Cloud quilting

Passing peaks
Sail silently under.
White armadas
Fusing in
Far oceans
Of undelineation

Winged time
Relentless
Gobbles seed seconds
Hours Husk float by
Pink silver edged
Disappearing down dying day

Bill Sutherland

WILDLIFE

Little bunnies hopping in the wood just by the park,
Squirrels in the tall trees chasing up and down the bark,
Pigeons cooing and pecking at the ground
Looking for morsels as they're strutting all around.
This wildlife seems free and gives me hope that is good,
Perhaps there is more in the seclusion of the wood.

Down by the glade amongst the undergrowth in holes
Live tiny little creatures such as shrews and mice and voles.
They don't come out till dusk, or dark or even black
When it's safe for them to do so, thinking they're safe from attack,
For there is a barn owl lives close by who needs to find a meal
And the threat of being caught by him is only all too real.

That's what life is all about, so we take it 'cause it's there,
Enjoying pleasures that life brings us be it badger, fox or hare.
The birds are also part of this great spectacle from above.
From the songbirds in the morning to the kestrel and the dove.
So let's hope it all continues giving joy without the strife
The simple pleasure of seeing them all and being part of life.

Gerard Oxley

AUTUMN GLORY

The birds begin to travel
As summer breathes its last
And autumn spreads her golden cloak
Upon the dewy grass

The colours of the trees are mingling
Red and brown
The green leaves slowly changing
Cascading to the ground

Earth yields her fruitful harvest
To gathering arms above
As I survey the splendour
Of this season that I love

The smell of wood smoke in the air
A chill wind gently roams
As this glorious chameleon
Sheds her warm and mellow tones

Yvonne Notholt

ENCHANTED WORLD

Snow-capped, elegant mountains inviting you to climb,
Icebergs floating gently, looking serene and so sublime.
Clouds drift past the moon, hiding it from view,
Smell the morning leaves, fresh tears of the dew.
Flowers gently swaying showing brilliant pigmentation,
Distinctive in design, and their variation.

Children running up and down with round shiny faces
Cow takes no notice, as in the field she grazes.
Shouts of joy and laughter playing favourite games
Scream and hide as thunder cracks, then comes the rain
Everything is still, apart from a sound of dripping
River full to the brim, her journey never ending.

Watching animals playing especially in the wild
Feeling the tightest cuddles from a little child
Simple things are special when you stop to think
First words from your son and his attempt to wink
Alluring and captivating as cobwebs in a breeze
Enchanting is our world, so full of things like these.

Denise Threlfall

THE FOUR SEASONS

S oft greens; yellows and blues blended together,
P urple tinting the round Scottish bens,
R ivers running silently through woodland,
I ncredibly long-legged foals are born,
N esting birds are grateful for twigs,
G entle ewes mother their lambs.

S cottish ephemeral summers,
U nder the sun nature smiles,
M ulticoloured flowers cover the verdant earth,
M oonlight casts an eerie light,
E ver-blue skies covered with wispy clouds,
R apidly, the sun evaporates dampness.

A utumnal browns; oranges and reds
U nveiled,
T rees shiver as they shed their leaves,
U nearthed are nuts as squirrels store them,
M ist and fog cover the hills,
N ature soon will be undisturbed.

W ild grouse leave spiky tracks in the snow,
I nsistant winds blowing determinedly,
N ights are long; mornings frosty,
T errifying shadows reach out to grab you,
E vergreen conifers stand alone, on
R olling Scottish mountains covered with snow.

Lucy Thomson (12)

SPRING IS IN THE AIR

Today the sun shines
And the air is so fresh
The birds start their singing
While they make their nest

Life has a new meaning
As spring is in the air
And courting and mating
Of animals starts everywhere

Life is so busy
As a spider spins a new web
And ants go off marching
As frogs lay their eggs

Bumble bees are humming
As flowers open out
The newly born babies
Are now hatching out

Lambs are so happy
And jump in the air
Other animals are waking
From the cold winters air

Butterflies are flying
All over the place
And life just becomes
One mighty race.

Susan Davies

SPINNING ROUND

The world spins round, the years spin round,
Ordered seasons following through
And as each season passes by
We watch as nature changes hue.

In spring the birds all flirt and groom,
Blue the sky though nights still cold,
But soon the flowers begin to bloom,
Mauve and yellow, blue and gold.

Trees in blossom, pink and white,
Warmer days in the month of May,
Soon June will come and we shall see
Roses fair all in array.

Now the summer flowers are blooming
In parks and gardens, colours bright,
Children playing, bees a-buzzing
And butterflies in joyous flight.

Then autumn comes, the leaves are changing
And as they gently flutter down
Children gather in their pockets
Shiny conkers richly brown.

Shorter days then come upon us,
Wintertime for fires that glow,
Frosty cobwebs on the hedgerow
And footsteps in the driven snow.

And so the year has spun around,
All the seasons passing by,
All the colours like a rainbow
Which shines across the evening sky.

Patricia Catling

SEASONS

W is for warm tucked up in my bed,
I is for the icicles on the roof above my head,
N is for nature's way of saying 'let's have a rest',
T is for turkey, traditionally the best.
E is for everything crisp and white with snow
R is reaching for your tissue to give your nose a blow.

S is for snowdrops swaying to and fro,
P is preparing the land, ready for the crops to grow,
R is for rabbits dancing with their mate
I is for insects crawling round the garden gate,
N is new growth - new life starts here
G is the glistening sun, making everything crystal clear.

S is for the sun shining down on me,
U is under the shade of an old apple tree,
M is making picnics to have in the park,
M is making music - the sweet music of the lark
E is the evenings - watching the sun go down,
R is for relaxing in your old dressing gown.

A is the apples as they fall off the tree,
U is for umbrellas as the rain falls down on me,
T is for trees as the leaves turn gold and rust,
U is understanding the birds will soon need a crust,
M is making sure all the delicate plants are in,
N is nature - the giver of everything.

Jayne Breden

IT'S THE WONDER OF SPRING

When the sun reaches down, from the heavens above
And God enshrouds the earth, in the warmth of His love
A new life in abundance, appears from all around
And tulips and daffodils, bring life to the ground
Crocuses and hyacinths, all join in the throng
With birds in the treetops, all joining them in song!

When the landscape is coated, in a carpet of green
And bluebells and primroses, appear on the scene
When rosebuds and blossom, decide to show their face
And caterpillars become butterflies, full of beauty and grace
When trees spread their branches, and unfold leaves of green
And the beauty of what surrounds us, is almost a dream

When the newly born lambs, begin to frolic and play
And the ice and the snow, has all melted away
When the water cascades, from the mountains above
And fills all the rivers, swelling them in flood
When the land is tilled, and the seeds of corn are sown
Making for a harvest, when our staff of life is born

When the hedgehogs and porcupines, appear in the light
And the hares and rabbits, all play out of sight
When the days become longer, and the dark is less seen
This wonder of nature, is a wonderful scene
There has to be a beginning, or we can't have an end
That's the miracle of nature, it's a God given blend
That is the wonder of spring!

Graham Thomas

SUMMER

In the pastel summer dawn
In the light of early morn
Birdsong choirs singing their lays,
Greeting lazy summer days.

Skylarks soaring in the sky,
Singing sweetly as they fly.
Doves are cooing and seagulls mewing,
Coming inland for their food, never enough for the hungry brood.

Spring has gone and summer has come
The lawn is in clover and bumble bees hum
The weeds grow faster than the flowers
The grass turns brown and we pray for showers.

Roses bloom in pinks and reds
Aubretia planted out in beds
Lavender-scented shady bowers,
For whiling away sweet summer hours.

Hazy, lazy summer days,
Drift away, but the memory stays
Of the pastel light of summer dawn
And strawberry teas out on the lawn.

Jean M Senior

THE SHADOWS OF THE TREES

The sunlit bank of green grass shines brighter than any emerald
Catching the eye, and lifting the heart.
The inky black shadows of the trees, dancing on the grass
Still for a moment, becoming an artist's perfection.
No human hand could draw so perfect and intricate a pattern.
Nature's instant photograph.
For an instant nothing disturbs the beauty of the scene
Then the breeze picks up, and once again the shadows dance.

Sarah Ollerenshaw

LIFE GOES ON

Darkening skies, threatening rain,
Not one day is ever the same,
See the lightning, hear the thunder,
Plans of a walk all gone asunder,

Rain tapping on the window pane,
Winds blowing, wildly insane,
Trees bending against their will,
How much longer for the wind to still,

The rain eases off, the wind much calmer,
The trees survived, their bark their armour
Branches denuded of their foliage,
Their lives cut short by the fierce storm's rage,

Clouds disperse, shadows are cast,
The first rays of sun, through at last,
Prisms of colour the rainbow unfolds,
A vision of wonder for us to behold,

The drooping flowers lift up their heads,
Water-logged in their garden beds,
Opening their petals in the warmth of the sun,
Their journey through life has just begun,

Rain and sun are what they need,
To help plants to mature and seed,
Nature's gifts we must employ,
To bring things to life, for us to enjoy,

From the cultivated plants in our garden,
Took from the greenhouse, and put out to harden,
To the wild flowers, called weeds by some,
Without nature's skills, no more would they come.

Glennis Horne

CLOUDS

I wonder if the clouds on high
Look down on me from a clear blue sky,
And I wonder if they know
That I desire to touch them so.
O clouds, if I could wallow,
And dance among your clefts of purple and yellow,
And feel the sun upon my face,
And linger in the limitless space,
Oh how happy I would be,
My soul and body in ecstasy!

Victor J Lawes

RED ROSES

Winter's echo has worn away,
As spring calls for the sun's warm ray,
With blossoms and birdsong and lambs at play.

Reflecting on the season now passed,
Nostalgic longing of memories lost,
I think of the things that I loved the most.

The wedding day with joyful poses,
Coldness showing in fingers and noses;
But best of all, my bouquet of red roses.

A special joy they gave to me,
A vow of love for all to see,
A winter's time of tranquillity.

Vows that I made that winter's day
May fade with time along the way.
But, I'll always remember my lovely bouquet.

Mildred Mayes

MARY'S ROBIN

Whilst working in her garden
She heard the softest call;
And looked around to see there -
A robin on the wall.

The sweetest feathered creature
That Mary could recall;
Intent to watch her labours -
The robin on the wall.

So close, and yet not frightened;
So chirpy, yet so small;
Just seeking human friendship -
That robin on the wall.

So often in her garden,
Though but three inches tall,
Sat her great companion -
Her robin on the wall.

For weeks she has not seen him;
No longer can enthral
To talk about the garden -
To robin on the wall.

Now always, in her garden,
Whatever may befall,
She looks - and hopes - and prays for -
Dear robin of the wall.

James R B Hinton

NATURE'S JOYS

I love woods and mossy places
Tucked away from open spaces
Dim and deep
And sunlight dappled
And in autumn
Bright crab-appled
Where voles by moonlight
Sit and eat
Clinging to branches
With tiny feet
Where birds in secret
Flit and flurry
In making nests
In springtime's hurry
Where striated frogs
And warty toads
Make their ways
By hidden roads

I love to watch
The winking
Moonlit pool
When silhouetted geese and coots
Move black, and bob about
Among excited ripples
Of buzzer feeding trout
Where passing owls do eerie hoot
And clash with honks
Of geese and coots

Paul Gamble

HANGING GARDENS

Gracefully hovering, as though suspended in mid air
They are tenderly nurtured with loving care

Filled with flowers of all shapes and forms
Just hang there, above bright coloured garden gnomes

Carefully pollinated by the busy bumble bee
Every colour of the rainbow is there to see

Hanging baskets come in all kinds of shapes
Leaves drape from their rims like royal capes

Blooms that were planted to grow a special way
Bow their heads to the sun, as though on display

Sunflowers that grow to enormous heights
In admiration, look down on these colourful sights

High on the walls, these hanging gardens hover
Contained in baskets, a must for any garden lover

Roy Hunter

THE ONCOMING OF SPRING

As gentle as a breath of wind
Spring bursts forth with great allure
Buds are sprouting on the trees
And birds sing sweetly everywhere
The sun shines warmly in the sky
With hopes of balmier days ahead
A precious season to be found
When all new life begins to form
Colour bursting in the fields
Thoughts of far off distant shores
Clear blue skies and long bright nights
Are not too distant now

L Caryll

IF I ONLY HAD TIME!

If I only had time
I'd climb a mountain,
If I only had time
I'd see the sea;
If I only had time
I'd watch the fountain,
And spend time just being me!

If I only had time,
I'd stop and listen;
I'd see the rainbow in the sky;
If I only had time,
I'd see cobwebs glisten,
And there'd be time for you and I.

If I only had time,
I'd hear birds singing;
I'd laugh and sing and dream and play,
If I only had time
I'd hear church bells ringing,
And go inside and kneel and pray.

If I only had time
I'd enjoy each moment
Of my life now here on earth;
I'd know what Jesus Himself meant,
When He told us of our own rebirth.

Betty Wilson

WREN IN A HEDGEROW

Tiny, brown bird, you remind me
of a mouse in the hedgerow,
ducking and darting from here to there,
scampering and scurrying everywhere.
If it wasn't for your tail
cocked high in the air,
I could easily mistake you
for a mouse.
You get distressed
as I near your nest
of tangled bracken.
But you needn't fear
or make such a fuss.
I wouldn't touch your
clutch of treasured eggs.
Go thee, Jenny Wren!
Go and hatch your
batch, such as you.

Brian Baxendale

FOUR SEASONS

Summer is the best time of year
The sun is out the sky is clear
Winter is setting in all around
Snow is falling on the ground
Autumn winds blow through the trees
To help with the loss of all their leaves
Spring is fine in the most beautiful way
Flowers blooming in the month of May.

Beverley Cooper

WHAT UNEARTHLY BEAUTY

Nature provides us with all sorts of
Beautiful things. There is the spring daffodil
And the equally beautiful tulip and in the
Summer the garden is full of beautiful
Flowers. There is first the rose, red, yellow,
Orange and white with the graceful lily
Showing herself to be as beautiful as any other.
Nature also provides beauty in a panorama of
Countryside with field and meadow,
Stream and hill showing how rare a
Visit to the country can be. And then
There are the beautiful sunsets in the west
With the sun painting all sorts of
Lovely pictures among the clouds,
Making us wonder at nature's diversity.

Thomas W Splitt

AUTUMN

Autumn leaves crimson and brown,
Falling, twirling, whirling down,
Covering the ground in a blanket of gold,
The wind blows strong, blustery and cold,
Summer is leaving, winter arriving,
Dormouse sleeping, hedgehog hiding,
Hips and haws, conkers and berries,
Out with the scarves, mittens and wellies,
A walk in the woods a squirrel we spy,
A skylark flying high up in the sky,
A rabbit scurrying into its hole,
Small little mounds the work of the mole,
Daylight is fading, evening is nigh,
The sun disappears, the moon's in the sky.

Margaret M Corder

ABIDING

Far above are the angels sighing?
Tears run like rivers along every lane.
A thousand sparkling diamonds fleeting
Raining showers against my window pane.

All waiting for a brighter morrow,
Lifted eyes seek the rainbow's flow.
Caring naught for unhappy hours
Wishing forever no cold winds blow.

Venus observed before the sunrise.
Clearly seen the morning or day star.
Fleeing clouds leaving perfect skies
Hopes and dreams true thus far.

Peeping from sunbeams yellow primroses,
Crocuses wake and close as if to pray.
Periwinkle vivid as shy violets
Dancing snowdrops greet the day.

Frolicking wings find a new pond,
Birdsongs echo or quiet as mice.
One tiny brilliant blue and yellow
Fights the larger for coconut and rice.

The water-hens are pretty neat
Taking off into the night
Huge swans majestic on the river
Much like twins of snowy white.

Never seen but heard a cuckoo call,
Viewing sweet memories of this land.
I believe the best has yet to come.
Think of a dove resting in God's hand.

Elsie Scrowther

NATURE

We cannot see the wind that blows,
We cannot see what makes grass grow,
We only know that God is there
He tries to prove it, do we care?

The little birds that fly above
Are there because of His great love,
He made all creatures great and small
He loves not one, He loves them all.

Wild flowers, they grow in different ways,
Some need wet soil, some need light shades,
Some need the cold, some need the sun
But all give pleasure when day is done.

White clouds, just drift along the way
Dark clouds are angry so they say,
Just make the time to stand and stare
Then you will know that God is there.

To each, He gave a gift to share
So let us show we really care,
By doing his work as well we may
And help each other on life's way.

Catherine Harrison

GOD'S LOVE

The mist evolved,
the wind, it howled,
it hooted and tooted,
the owl in the tree,
the wings of an eagle fly high,
there is the flutter of a magpie.
The gentle swaying of trees,
and the sting of the bees.
All mean it is real,
Creation does deal,
all its things out,
when we are out and about,
and beneath the still rocks above,
the stars tell of God's love,
and scream it aloud.

Julie Allison

SNOW

Little snowflakes soft and white,
Flutter down in the dead of night.

Make the children's faces glow,
As they frolic in the snow.

Then send them in to cosy fires,
Where they play until they tire.

Off to bed now up the stairs,
Where God will listen to their prayers.

Once more children safe and sound,
Until the morning comes around.

Susan Goldsmith

COUNTRY SCENE

The rural scene is ruddy and raw
With blackberry, hip, and haw
On the hedgerows there displayed
A bounty of wild fruit, with branches weighed
Ripe for picking, jam to be made

The seagulls follow the plough to find
Food for them of any kind
Shadowing its progress down the field
Seeking for what it can yield
for them

The shepherd whistles to his dog
To round up the sheep
He checks his flock his vigil to keep
The new-born lambs stay by mum
To keep safe when the day is done

The vixen is on the prowl
For any food, meat, or fowl
It has its cubs to feed
And see to their every need

And so life goes on
To every animal, and bird in song
As God planned and made for us life long
Our world, our life, our all
We have to answer to His call
With love

D M Brown

SUMMER HARVEST

Blackberry picking.
Faint threads of autumn
slip through passing clouds
paving the way for cooler days ahead.
A bramble hedge holds fast its secret store,
just out of reach
until low branches, laden with glossy fruit
offer up their harvest
close enough to draw blood.

The sun appears.
End of summer thoughts evaporate
as cardigans now hastily removed
show deeply tanned, sea-salted arms.
Wasps appear from nowhere.
The sheltered field, redolent of early June
is full of expectation
and baskets overflow with ripened berries.
Summer lingers.

Vanessa Miles

ABOVE A TREE

Above a tree,
I float,
Listening to the sounds,
Bluebells all around,
A blue and purple sea,
Through the trees the sun breaks through,
Lighting up the ground,
Birds' glorious songs lift my heart,
As I float above the tree,
Getting higher and higher,
The blue sea fades away.

Laura Benbow (9)

THE SUMMER GARDEN

The sweet heady smell of honeysuckle,
The beauty of marguerites,
The blue and pink of fuschia,
That's struggling with the heat.
The pansies are there but tiny,
The laveteria's simply huge,
The phlox and chives lie side by side
With growth, they will probably fuse.
It is in this enclosed garden,
Where the hovering bees' humming sound
Is often the only noise we hear . . .
That nature has turned around.
No more the barren hedges,
Filled with layers of snow,
No more the struggling, pushing buds,
For summer is here once more.

Jeanette McDonald

ONCE

Once this land was lush and green,
The mighty oak, a joy to be seen.
But now this land is dry and stark,
The oak's lost its leaves, bare of bark.
Global warming I'm told, there's no solution,
Until we get to grips with world pollution.
So come dear friends, let us all try,
To save our world, not let it die.
Let's do our best, it's our collective duty,
To keep our world a thing of beauty.
Once peoples of this world unite,
We'll save our world from its sorry plight.

John Milne

IT WAS WELL

The air was filled with merry song.
A scent was in the breeze.
We walked along the woodland path
Together so at ease.

The butterflies just hovered
Above the grass so tall,
Whilst nature wore her greenest dress
To grace the summer ball.

The magpie strutted just ahead,
Inspecting all around.
I gazed with joy at all I saw
And cherished each sweet sound.

My dog had bounded down the bank
And splashed in cooling stream.
Such beauty lay in everything.
I stood as in a dream.

The water flowed so peacefully,
The fish all nimbly played.
Around the reeds the ducklings swam
And gentle ripples made.

I'd left the other world behind.
It lay far out of sight,
For here was beauty; here was peace.
Here was the world's delight.

The sun shone down to bless each one
And cast its magic spell,
Whilst God I'm sure looked down on all
And saw that it was well.

John Christopher Cole

RICHES

Brilliant yellow glistening in sunlight,
Precious as gold
Bursting forsythia.

Deep rich purple, faces uplifted,
Soft touch as velvet,
Thoughtful pansies.

Blue like the sea, still as the night,
Beautiful as sapphires,
Carpet of bluebells.

Delicate as lace, pale green in colour,
Wave in the wind,
Uncurling ferns.

Enjoying a bath, singing his song,
Jet black like ebony,
A solitary blackbird.

Colourful poppies dance in the grasses,
Rubies red,
A wonderful sight.

Climbing the trellis, white scented jasmine,
Oil so costly,
Perfume so rare.

Garden of treasures, rich as a mine,
Winter a memory,
Springtime has come.

Pamela Stoner

SPRINGTIME

Good old Mother Nature,
she always does her thing.
Springtime has arrived
and the birds begin to sing.
Tulips, crocus, daffodils,
pop up to say hello,
bringing pretty colours
and as the wind begins to blow,
they sway about so gently
as if dancing in the breeze
and all the old bare trees
have been renewed with fresh green leaves.
Lambs and calves are being born,
now that springtime's here,
and there is no doubt to me
that it's my favourite time of year.

Nicola Taylor (13)

HEDGE PARSLEY

Sweet summer there
When hedgerows puff out lace
No windows bare to screen
But curtains hung with care
Soft-spread with grace
Fair-backed with green.
A living lace
Begot of earth and sun and breeze
Sweet-washed by Mother Nature
At nature's pace
With nature's ease.

Norah Mitchell

HE WHO CARES

You gave us your love and we know
that You care and you listen to
our little prayers, we seem to ask
such a lot from You, like wealth, health,
and happiness too, we ask You to help
others as well, so where would we be if
You were not there to listen to our little
prayer, You open Your arms to gather
us in, those who are good and those
who have sinned You have no
favourites at all, and You love all
creatures great and small so
thank you God for all that You do
and for listening to our prayers
too where would we be
without You

Olivia Stokes

A THUNDER STORM

I hear the rumble of thunder and see the lightning streak
Not for me a hiding place do I ever seek
I enjoy a thunder storm as it rages on and on
People say I must be weird, others, there's something wrong
The rain is tapping softly on my window pane
Thunder rumbles louder as lightning strikes again
As I pull back my curtains to look at the sky
I see people with umbrellas quickly running by
The sky is a blur there's only dark cloud
Another crack of thunder ever so loud
Now the rain is lashing down
I watch it bounce upon the ground
I should be thinking of the dangers it brings
Instead I think nature's a wonderful thing.

Barbara Ramsey

TREES OF LIFE

Trees of the forest, strong and true
Your changing seasons all year through
Touch our lives with hope anew,
Fresh promise everywhere.

Tall and stately you all stand
Marching like soldiers throughout the land,
To the heavens you hold your hands
While birds rest in your hair.

Seasons come and quickly go,
Winter's frost with ice and snow
Precedes spring's new life aglow,
Then summer's sunshine fair.

Autumn follows, shining bright,
Glowing with such radiant light;
Why has man caused so much blight
While we just stand and stare?

Glorious, yes - essential too
To help us live our lifetime through;
'Tis true that we shall never see
A poem lovely as a tree:
Please God, make us care.

Joyce Pither

SNOWFLAKES FALLING

Falling gently without a sound
Quickly covering all the ground
Coating everything it touches
With little flakes it firmly clutches

Trees and houses get a dusting
Like a duvet spreading, busting
Across the ground it swiftly spreads
Covering grass and flowerbeds

It brings a silence of its own
You suddenly seem to be alone
The cold it tends to put at bay
The warmth under the snow does lay

Then one day the thaw begins
Melting the snow to icy things
Slushy, slippy wet and grey
Until another snowy day

Elizabeth Hobson

WINTER

Winter spread her cloak around
Icy fingers touch the ground.
Trees stand tall and bare
Branches reaching into cold air.

Nestling in the roots below
Seedlings wait; in time to grow.
Fields though green, have a bleaker look,
Water ice cold in that babbling brook.

Frost is upon us as days go by,
Moonlight brighter in the darken sky.
Spiders' webs so neat and fine
Hanging like lace, they shimmer and shine.

Soon the earth will be covered with snow
Keeping warm the life below.
Icicles hang from window ledges,
Berries fill the trees and hedges.

Small animals hide themselves away
To sleep and wait; for the coming day,
When Mother Nature changes her coat once more
And *spring* is knocking on our door.

Iris Taylor

THE CHANGING SCENES

What a wondrous sight it is
To behold
Autumn in all her splendour begins
To unfold.
Leaves that flutter in
The breeze.
Float down gently from tall
Stately trees.
Softly softly without
A sound.
Making patterns on
The ground.
Rich in colours that
Are mellow
Shades of golden browns
And yellow.
Swirling leaves
All around
Gather together in
Leafy mounds.
All in time the scene
Will change
As only Mother Nature
Can arrange.

Gloria Wilkes

MUSHROOMS - TENDER PALE AND PURPLE GREEN

Under the shadow of the Himalayan range,
Just about at the time of break of dawn,
The twilight mist still exists,
But the dusk had long been gone.

Sometimes the rain is somewhat hesitant,
Turning the air cool, fresh and fragrant.

Washed all night with gentle silvery moonlight,
Clusters of mushrooms spring up here and there,
To welcome sunrise struggling through the night.

Fields and forests littered with them,
As if stars had fallen from their den.

Excited children run and scream,
To see the sight of mushrooms,
Tender pale and purple green.

Yet man is now in a position better than ever,
A crop of mushrooms to grow, bigger and clever.
With new inventions at his behest,
Life on earth He can lay to rest.

Up and down the earth - east and the west,
Fresh mushrooms will grow on rotten flesh.

Only then, there will be no
Excited child to run and scream,
To see the sight of mushrooms,
Tender pale and purple green.

M Yaqub Mirza

SPRING 1945

Down the shafts of sunlight from spring's unclouded sky,
Happy thoughts come tumbling and little breezes sigh,
With sweet content, and sing a song on soft and mellow key,
Of sunlit hills and blossomed vales crowned by summer sea.

The daffodils are nodding as with a blaze of gold
We find their flowery carpet beneath our feet unrolled
Can it be only yesterday the world was bleak and bare
And winter's wind-tossed raven locks had snowflakes in her hair.

The earth was filled with thunder and cries of human strife,
'Til spring with rippling laughter came with new and springing life.
Oh, weary world look up, look up, and smile on heaven above
Cast down the bitter cup of hate and drink the joy of love.

Bring home the weary traveller, begrimed with smoke and toil
To find the joys of springtime on this beloved soil.

Margaret Morrow

THE AWAKENING

Winter's retreat yields the eager desire
To see fields of ice
Turn to fields of fire
Ignited by embers made flaming through need
Of nature to blossom
The bud and the seed

And when final fragments of frost are disowned
The seasoned pretender
Lays claim to the throne
And embroiders a delicate pattern so fine
That heralds the arrival
Of vivid springtime

David Harrison

SPRING

I look through my window what do I see
Bluebells dancing in the breeze happily
Tulips standing proud and bold
although the weather is fairly cold
But then maybe the day will unfold
and the sun show its rays of gold
Dandelions yellow and bright
Cherry blossoms a lovely sight
Petals strewn all around
like confetti on the ground
Birds flying from tree to tree
tweeting their songs so merrily
People walking here and there
Maybe instances of the day compare
Showers falling they come and go
Raindrops sparkle all aglow
All the gems in the world can't compare
With the beauty of nature we all share

Jessica Looke

WITHOUT A PADDLE

Have you ever thought
How it would be
If there wasn't a sun
And there wasn't a sea?
The sky would have a great big hole
And all the stars would fall in
And all the rivers flowing along
Would have nowhere to end in,
So all the people who follow the stars
Their fame and fortune to seek
Would follow the rivers meandering along
And find themselves up the creek.

Briallen Richards

THE ROSE

Petals roses red
pink and white
Just like beauty
At its delight

Soft fragrance elegant
grabbed painful
Just like you can't
grab love

Growth development
cared for
Petals falling
dawning is near

They come in
summer
Educational, development
Beautiful

Thorns surround
their beauty
Thorns of dismissal
held on to anchor

Don't touch the rose
let it die
and don't leave people
like me asking why

So if you see a
rose touch not
The thorns they prick
You once forgot

C McAloon

SPRING

Spring is here with winter gone
the clouds have passed, the sun has shone
our timely friends that burrowed deep
are now awake from winter's sleep.

Spring is here, the swallows have come
revelling in our English sun
they have come from far away
so much to do in their time of stay.

Spring is here it is time to sow
if we want our seeds to grow
for if we sow, we then must reap
to fill our stores with winter's keep.

Spring is here it is time for birth
the sun has warmed the cold dark earth
lambs are frisking here and there
no sight could ever be so fair.

Spring is here with gardens agleam
children play in the nearby stream
on the banks the bluebells grow
with stately heads they are aglow.

Spring is here but time moves on
June has come, the days are long
as seasons change and clouds pass by
so to spring we say goodbye.

Daisy Cooper

THE LITTLE STREAM

By verdant hill and glen you come,
Child of the waterfall;
A whisper in the quiet wood
Where oak and elm stand tall.

You sing with thrush - or nightingale
Your mystic, sweet refrain:
What do you care if skies be grey,
Friend of the wind and rain!

You wind your way to secret haunts
By bracken, moss and fern;
Perchance to meet a kindred stream -
But never to return!

The wild flowers on your sunny banks
Delight the honeybee,
While birds in ecstasy of song
Look down from every tree.

O little silver stream, wind on,
A-sparkle in the sun,
Until you reach your destiny,
Where deep dark waters run.

Patricia McGavock

GARDEN IN WINTER

Away from bustling streets, the sheltered ground,
Covered in snow, lies like a chrysalis.
Frozen bushes, leafed with clinging flakes,
And touched by the pale sun, border smooth lawns,
Spread white, untrodden, round the house.
Tomorrow the demolition men come in.
They'll clear the site to plant an office block.

Brian Sandwell

HIGHLIGHT AND HARMONY

Creator's glorious rainbow binding earth to heaven,
Heralding St David's Day, daffodil, and Eastertide,
Interlocking past to present 'bow within the cloud' (Gen: 1.13)
Father's covenant of mercy. Love personified,
'For He has blessed us all in the fullness of His grace' (John 1.16)
Praise and thanksgiving imparting light within to brace
Responsive need with fellowship to others surely gives
Heartening sense of worship as Harvest Service lives
In cherished memory of fruit and flower round pulpit croft,
Red berried boughs and pampas grass hosannas wave aloft,
Coppergold as tapered candles organ pipes that ringing
Majestic paean or pastoral embroidery to our singing . . .
Right here by my windows now the sturdy chestnut tree
Stands weatherwise to winter, snow and rain,
Candleflowers in glad profusion ere this verdant beauty of summer greenery!
A pair of lively squirrels' home is in the tree trunk too
In chasing rivalry with robin and a butterfly in view!
I had an anxious moment when a red car seemed to be
Right on a racing squirrel but he got by fearlessly!
And memories in earlier chapters happily recalls
Our home and garden flowers, greenhouse with tomatoes,
Runner beans on garden wall,
Highlight and harmony
In life His light conveys
Blest family relationship
Through all our ways.

Iris Lewis

AUTUMN

The grass feels soft
Beneath my feet
The heavenly frangrance
Smells strong and sweet.

Harebells jangle
And dance in the breeze
I can hear Mother Nature
Shaking her keys.

She's preparing to lock
The summer away
For no one season
Comes to stay.

Leaves will turn
To a burnished gold
And autumn's beauty
Will softly unfold.

Lacy cobwebs
Traced with dew
Swirling mists
To hide the view.

Of wine red hips
Of berries bright
Of autumn's glory
In a mystic light.

Sue Saxby

IN SURREY

Ah! What beholds my wandering gaze,
That travels through a mist and haze,
Until it rests on yonder heights,
A scene of wonder and delights.

For long I feast my eyes and see,
Each blade of grass, each woodland tree,
Each vale and hill each flower of hue,
Each bird and beast that holds my view.

'Tis nature's hand alone has wrought,
This charm which I for long have sought,
And lo awakes within my breast,
A quiet calm a peaceful rest.

Into my utmost being fills,
A sense of ease from cares and ills,
From earthly fears my heart doth flee,
And I think of Him who gave to me.

So may I then my course pursue,
With cheerful heart and hope anew,
'Tis nature that had bid me see,
How very kind He is to me.

And if I'd wish in my small way,
His loving kindness to repay,
Then He must see in me,
All the beauty all the grace, of bird and woodland tree.

Ann Moiser

FLOWER POWER

What is this magic force
that makes things come to life,
year by year, without fail, always on course,
it's gentle Mother Nature
never ceasing to surprise,
as her beauty she unfolds
slowly, before our eyes.
She slips in like a sunbeam,
as quiet as morning dew,
unfurling flowered carpets
all a different hue,
trees turn into great umbrellas,
leaves a hundred shades of green,
what a sense of order,
an event that must be seen.
So, see, hear, breathe it in,
the year's finest hour,
this is what's meant, in every sense,
the meaning of flower power.

Audrey Packman

COLOURS OF SUMMER

Soft in the hazy mist
the colours of summer
caught in the warm glow
of the season's sun.

Violet, lilac, peach and rose
yellow orange on it goes
mixed with shades of many greens
herbal gardens, runner beans.

All the flowers, bushes and trees
the constant buzz of the honey bees
the baby birds in their nests
indulging in their parents' tastes of garden pests.

And we too! Humans all
that live to hear summer's call
will tan ourselves while baring all.

T M Harden

SPURN

Broken backed against the salt air
planed and stunted,
bark knuckles
blackened,
resolute.

Dune grass sentries beckon the wave
razor lipped and sure,
sand marshals,
building,
drowning.

Spattered and dappled with wheeling
birds, the grey sea
fret sponges,
squeezes,
wets.

Gorse and sea lavender shiver on
the spit in the heavy
breath, riding
the white
caps.

Ian Gent

SUN

Here you come burn-ball,
orange eye,
hot light
over the mud-churned land,
my cloud warrior,
devoted friend,
wheat-warmer.
On the edge of every bud,
birds rise up,
waters break,
my spirit glows.
Swirling fist
you blind me
with a thousand of yourself.

David Wallace

CLEAN EARTH

Tall trees,
Grey rocks
Round and bumby.
Green grass,
And
Clean water . . .

People should
Put paper wrappers
In a bin,
Or if there is
No bin;
Put it in your pocket.
I like clean parks!

Scott Lewis

YOUR WORLD

Tender
Raw to memory
Bleeding
Your sky

Blades
Succulent life
Clasping
Your hair

Clouds
Scattered letters
Holding
Your world

Leaves
Stir into breath
Yielding
To your tune

I wring my heart
My essence
Seeps through
Your earth

You wring your heart
Tinge
The petals
Flesh

No need to fear
My tears disperse
Lost in you

Marcella Cullen

GERMINATION

The seeds in the egg box
faithfully sprayed
were hidden from view
only dry earth displayed.

So I in impatience
with nothing to gain
plan to throw them away
- much to my shame

For there in my absence
they have taken root,
a compost pincushion
for each delicate shoot

Nature's clock cannot be forced
however hard we reason
every living force on earth
is subject to its seasons.

Our nature's to behave this way
with time to reap and sow
and so we should allow the time
for each of us to grow

Chrissy Smith

SEASONS

As the amber haze of autumn
Highlights the hills once more
And the blue grows much darker
Where the waves reach the shore

We remember the wilds of winter
Snow stretched to the water's edge
Winds directly from the Arctic
Howled their biting pledge

Then the gentleness of springtime
When peeping primroses appear
Before the blaze of rhododendron
Splashes colour everywhere

The long warm nights of summer
When the sun barely leaves the sky
Days calm and clear and golden
All too fleetingly pass by

Vivien Heather

THE NORTH WIND

Winter wind you seek me out
As you sought my kin before
The flesh succumbs to your sharp edge
But my soul is keened the more.

Keened to wrestle to and fro
Across your terrible waste
Paying you in life and limb
To sate a murderer's taste.

A cavernous maw of snow and ice
Clamps on this land of mine
Locking crops and beasts and men
Into an endless mime.

The sun at last claws up the sky
Mile after endless mile
And slackens your harsh glacial jaw
Into an idiot's smile.

And then we shout and run and leap
As you slide and sink to the sea
For I am lost in a warm embrace
When the soil comes back to me.

David Tas

THE BEGINNING OF SPRING

Spring is sprung, we've heard it before,
Daffodils dance by every door.
The air's getting warmer, oh what a treat!
The ducks are hungry for something to eat.

At weekends there's activity all round,
People are sewing grass seed or digging the ground.
Cars are being washed at fearsome pace,
Getting thin for the summer is everyone's race.

The birds seem more lively they cheep louder now,
That beautiful new calf belongs to Daisy the cow.
The lambs appear as if out of the blue,
And wag their tails as lambies do!

The trees are changing as green buds burst through,
The soil's heating up and seedlings peep out too!
Lawns are cut and trimmed without delay.
'Summer's coming at last' we all say.

Tulips, wallflowers and sweet peas grow.
How does it happen? - Only God does know.
As if by magic plants are switched on,
And every day brings a brand new dawn.

Some of the changes we do see,
But many are hidden from you and from me.
Our Maker has made such a wonderful place.
Springtime is wonderful, it's so full of grace.

Ruth L Ironside

OUR FEATHERED FRIENDS

Follow the birds as they soar quite high
Flying around and around in the sky
Looking out for any food on the ground
Turning in circles around and around
Swooping sometimes to pick up some food
Then flying away to some distant wood

Spring is a time when birds are quite busy
Busily building their nests until they're quite dizzy
Awaiting in pairs for their new recruits
Although at first they appear to be in shell suits
Sitting and waiting and keeping them warm
Guarding and caring to keep them from harm

Only a couple of weeks they've to wait
Before father looks after his chicks with his mate
Fetching and carrying the food one by one
Waiting until all the feeding is done
Before it is time for them to have food
Without bringing it all back just for the brood

With wings strongly feathered they are fully grown
It is time for the chicks to have up and flown
It's a hazardous task but they must keep on trying
Flapping and jumping until they are flying
When they are flying and are now in the air
The nest looks quite empty and totally bare

After lessons of flying around and around
Parents then take them down onto the ground
To show them the items that they can eat
And how to use bird baths and keep themselves neat
At last the chicks have come into their own
Sadly leaving the parents temporarily alone

Wendy Winslet

AMOUR EXCELLENCE!

An intimate affair with nature,
An ancient, shrouded pathway maybe.
Now cloaked by other's notions of *love*.
Not of the natural and the real,
But of the dominate word,
With its images of distortion.

Words that do not exist in the womb,
Only a stimulating, tingling array of senses,
While awaiting expulsion into the world.
To grow and to learn within its mystical cycle.
Rocking us with its tidal sways,
Embracing us with its rhythmic beat.
Radiating a *knowledge* that awaits to rejoin us,
On the other side.

Nature's forever a faithful partner,
No promises, no betrayal, no lies.
Dwelling above the mundane plain of man.
Where a universal level of existence and reason
Can be reached,
That's pure, unadulterated, and free.

'Tis only so, when we retain or can re-kindle the vision.
Ours as children,
Knowing that this *is* as it should be!
Not snatched from us, and tainted,
Obscured, and denied, in order to conform.
Leaving us forever grieving for . . .

Sunsets that form horizontal rainbows,
Tantalising aromas to warm our spirit,
Erotic caresses bringing quivering pulsations,
And melodies that comfort our heart.
Whispering seductively to our soul,
Entwining the one with the other,
Into becoming the whole.

M D Dance

AN OLDE SPRING TALE

I once heard a merry tale
of spring days I was told,
No rain, no moon, no sun, no hail
they spoke in days of olde,

A princess; Lucy who began to cry
her tears they turned to rain,
Hence never from that day did she die
as the princess felt no pain,

Lucy became the God of Spring
no man would marry her,
A band of gold, a wedding ring
just to call him Sir,

The flowers arose and came to life
beauty became so fair,
Princess Lucy was the new spring wife
now with rainbow coloured hair,

Gareth Smith

MOONLIGHT ON THE SEA

Why doesn't someone write a poem
About moonlight on the sea?
Someone who knows telling words -
Far more than you or me -

The glint and the gleam of it
The sheer, lovely dream of it

The smooth, silken feel of it
The is-it-really-real? of it

The magic and the mystery
The stories told in history

The calm and the balm of it
The singing like a psalm of it

The stillness and the shine of it
The heady, sparkling wine of it

The moving of the waves of it
The dark, mysterious caves of it

The round, shining ball of it
The peace over all of it -

If only I could float along that silver way
In a little, silent boat right out across the bay -

Would it be like the rainbow's end
Where colours fade and die?
Or would there be a magic place
Between the sea and sky?

If only I could sail across that silvery sea
Would there be a mermaid waiting there for me?

Isobel Marion Morton

CAMBRIDGE SNOW

It's better this way,
formulae in low relief.
Unique.
Every crystal,
a masterpiece.
Perfection in ice.

Etched by,
Some maniacal pavement artist,
who did not stop at the curb
but clung to buildings
trees and post,
sculpting bulging lids
on this amorphous city.

Benjamin F Jones

NINE SECONDS FLAT

My wildlife friendly garden stays alive with birdsong,
With dawn and evening chorus and chirruping, all day long.

Until, just for a few seconds, about two years ago,
Nature played an unbelievable, highly charged brief dramatic show.

Solemn golden-beaked blackbird gave his Pink! Pink! Pink! Sharp cry.
Then past my kitchen window, a ruffled kestrel plummeted by.

No prey caught, he stood frowning, with disbelief upon his face,
But nothing had prepared him for what would next take place.

Suddenly, a gyrating mass of cacophonous sparrows, rising as one,
Filled the air with anger.
Kestrel fearful, frowned and was gone.

Peace returned, leaving me incredulous. Had I *really* seen that?
Potential prey rallied, foe dismissed, in nine seconds flat.

Annalise Usher

LOOKING AROUND

Spring brings miracles by the score.
Wherever we turn, we see more and more.
Look at the snowdrops, so fragile are they,
Yet one of the first to see light of day.

Crocuses, mauve, yellow and white,
Have managed to pop up to see the light.
Then come daffodils, stately and tall
Yes, it is spring which heralds them all.

Tiny buds to new foliage waiting to burst,
Bulbs to be flowers, how they thirst.
When God in his power gives the word,
Then the call of nature will be heard.

Primroses and violets we shall find,
If we walk in the woods, with bluebells lined.
Celandines and buttercups scattered around,
Daisies too in the fields abound.

Remember too, the birds on the wing,
They get busy when they sense it is spring.
Collecting bits of this and that,
They must, of course, *beware the cat.*

So just look around, and over the fields,
See the wonder of what the earth yields.
Dark winter has gone, now we can cope,
Hope springs eternal - Spring brings Hope.

Doris Huff

BRAVE NEW SUMMER

At the first glimpse of a breaking bud,
I feel a surging of the blood,
And I get impatient for:

Greenness, butterflies, flowers and . . .
        Heat exhaustion.

Deckchairs, dark glasses, choc-ices and . . .
        Greenfly.

Fresh lettuce, ice-cubes in drinks,
Bare feet, watering cans and . . .
        Sticking to the bed-sheets.

Actually wanting to get up in the morning,
Corn poppies, white clouds, picnics,
Warm rain and . . .
        Wet cheese.

Oh summer don't hang back.
Be brave;
Ambush me at the end of April
And hold me to ransom,
Until autumn pays up
With showers of glittering gold.

Geoff Carder

TREE AT NIGHT

I like to think of the fruits on the tree at night,
ripening quietly like small hearts
each one beating softly with its own life.
In the daylight the fruits become the property of others,
of greedy eyes.
They hang perilously, vulnerable, exposed.
But at night the soft dark air circles around gently,
the moon pours her secret metals down.
Ancient light, cool and knowing,
lies with the blue black darkness
casting its own mysterious illumination.

Sally Goolden

AUTUMN MEETS WINTER

The leaves of gold drop to the ground,
Over fields the mist lies low,
Frost creeps up without a sound
Rehearsing for the snow.

Naked trees, tinged with frost
They sparkle in the chill,
Colourful blooms forever lost
As the air grows colder still.

Animals nestle down all snug
Asleep until the thaw,
The snow arrives and forms a rug
Across the country's floor.

Longer nights and shorter days,
Fires blazing in the grate,
Spring will blossom in many ways
There won't be long to wait.

A Turner

ENVIRONMENTAL STUDIES

Schools teach children about Nature
This subject can be a lot of fun
It is now called Environmental Studies
And must begin in Primary One.
As young children are so interested
In what is going on all around
From the Ecology and the Ethos
To all things growing in the ground.
Pupils are not just passengers
It is surprising what they already know.
So, by simply fostering their interest
This is helping their wee minds to grow.
I spy with my little eye
May be rather an old-fashioned game
Parents too can play it with them
Soon they can give everything a name.
Teachers now take them out to the playground
Or out into the neighbourhood each week
As schools encourage this type of activity
Another favourite game is still *Hide and Seek.*
In places where there are trees or bushes
Naming the ones they already know
If possible planting bulbs or seeds
So that they can *watch their own garden grow.*
By training them young to be earth caretakers
Time will have been wisely invested
The seeds of knowledge that have been sown
Will flourish and keep them interested.

Mary Anne Scott

BEAUTY

There's beauty all around us for all of us to see
There's beauty in the hedgerow and in a tall fir tree
There's beauty in a hillside and in the sky above
There's beauty in the moonshine when we look at it with love
There's beauty in the sunshine high up in the skies
Just see it rise in Palma you won't believe you eyes

The most beautiful place I love to be
Is strolling peacefully by the sea
I love to see the waves as they lap up on the shore
And the pleasant smell of seaweed I really do adore

To think all this beauty was made by the Lord above
With a lot of imagination and a whole lot of love

Kathleen M Egan

SUMMER STORM

Flattened, grey colour-washed skies,
Their weight sustained by branches of trees,
Are brushed by gathering, rain-laden clouds
In the sudden surge of an up-springing breeze.

Giving voice to fury in a blackening anger,
They roll and clash in a thundering clangour,
The light of fire from a murderous eye
Streaks the heavens to terrify.
Tears of rage descend in a spate,
Making the earth, below, vibrate.

Then suddenly, the world is still,
Suspended in time for an endless moment
Before the storm is past and forgotten,
And the sun shines again in the hope of atonement.

B Gordon

THE FUTURE OF NATURE

Rolling hills
Flowing streams
Clean, fresh air
Another dream

Tall grey buildings
Concrete blocks
Long, winding roads
Thick with smog

Bright, blue sky
Green, green grass
Brilliant sun
All is past

Honking horns
Ringing bells
Dirty streets
Dirty smells

What have we done?
Who is to blame?
We're all indifferent
But we're all the same
We're all to blame!

Gemma Johnson

ICY MORSEL

Falling frosty sparkling flakes
Cascading down onto the icy lakes

Gathering snow from all around
Forming your body, I'll be bound

Trussed up in your splendid grandeur
I can't be sure about my candour

Because the temperature is set to rise
My, aren't you in for a big surprise

As I opened my eyes and rushed to the window
I could almost hear your disdainful cries.

For lying there, heaped upon the garden path
A mangled straw hat, beside a moth-eaten scarf

I tried to warn you that you weren't immortal
But just an icy little morsel.

Created one cold snowy day, and then
Slowly doomed to fade away.

G Crumpton

SUMMER

Strawberries and cream,
Scent of a rose,
Cricket on the green,
A sprinkling hose,
Golden yellow corn
Soon ready to reap,
Lazy sunbathers
Fast asleep!

Joan Sabin

MY FAVOURITE THINGS

The liquid sound of a nightingale,
Or a long necked graceful swan.
A robin redbreast on the path
Blue-tits in Hawthorn hedges.

Carpets of bluebells in the wood
And furry pussy willows.
Meadows full of buttercups,
Or primroses in a dell.

Crocus, purple, white and golden.
Daffodils in profusion.
Forsythia and lavender
Roses and honeysuckle.

Bubbling streams, fast flowing rivers,
Mountain peaks and smooth green hills.
Lakes and waterfalls cascading
Craggy rocks and shady woods.

Dramatic winter morning skies,
Glistening frost on the branches.
Thunderstorms with lightning flashes
Superb, colourful sunsets.

These are some of my favourite things,
Which I enjoy each day.
God's intricately created world,
Wonderful to me.

Joyce Wakefield

NATURE'S WOODLAND JOURNEY

Tall growing trees reaching up to the sky,
Leaf covered branches outstretched, spreading wide,
Shafts of bright light on the leaves, how they gleam
Like small sun drenched waves of the deepest blue green.

The breeze now moves gently and slowly around,
Rustling leaves way up high and those on the ground.
Sighing its way through the long summer days,
Bending young saplings, its true strength now betrays.

As time passes on, trees soon wear autumn crowns
Of red and of gold and the deepest of browns.
Cool winds moan thro' forests and down country lanes,
Shaking leaves from the branches, like soft golden rain.

Soon the ice and the snow a huge white cloak make,
The sea then becomes a great silver lake.
No sound, as the giants still sleep peacefully on,
Waiting quietly, so patiently, for winter's cold to be gone.

Here at last, comes a warm breeze that's so welcome, will creep
To wake up the tall trees from their long dreamless sleep.
Their branches move slowly, the whole forest awake
And the new blue green waves, once again start to break.

Brenda Rose Firth

THE MIRACLE OF NATURE

The natural world is governed by the vagaries of the seasons
And each one is important for a multitude of reasons.
The spring and summer epitomise the blossoming of life
While in autumn and in winter we witness hibernation rife.
Spring may be the finest season which we enjoy on this earth
For, in all of nature's life forms, we begin to see new birth.
Spring flowers bloom and, all around, expectancy's in the air
And leaves and blossom cover trees which winter had laid bare.
The sun in summer has the heat to nurture nature's stock.
It also brings refreshing rain to quench its thirsty flock.
Summer sees the growth of the new-births from the spring.
The time when all the crops do grow. No wonder wild birds sing!
Autumn heralds the approach of potential winter sights,
Bringing shorter days and the longer, colder nights;
Autumnal colours from deep red to various shades of brown;
With strong winds *getting up* and the spent leaves falling down.
Winter has frost as a feature and, sometimes, a blanket of snow.
Hibernation is nature's answer, in the lands where cold north winds blow.
Food for wildlife is at a premium with everything laid bare
And it's a real fight for survival to try to get one's share.
Spring starts nature's annual cycle at the Vernal Equinox
When the dormant life of winter, nature instinctively unlocks.
The growth of animals, plants and trees are beautiful to behold
Until the Autumnal Equinox begins to turn green leaves to gold.
The quality of human life is enhanced by nature's miracle
Of rebirth and re-awakening, because nature is empirical.
The lambs at play, the birds that sing, bring pleasure at every age.
The blossom and flower gardens are backdrops for the world's stage.
So, whatever nature proffers always treat with veneration
Then this miracle can be enjoyed by every generation.

John W Skepper

THE WORLD ABOUT US

Where do all the seasons go, asks the owl in the tree,
As primulas and hyacinths surge through the frosted ground,
And the golden bells of the daffodil appear, such a joy to see,
As March comes in with a blustery sound.

Where does the spring go to, asks the wind of March,
As it makes way for April's showers,
And Easter's blooms bring dreams of a new start,
As soon the air is filled with the sweet smell of lavender's flowers.

Roses slumber the warm days away, painted with colours of every hue,
As summer once again comes to call,
But all too soon autumn comes into view,
As motionless leaves stand poised to fall.

Where has autumn gone, asks the leaves as they wait to fall,
And the first icy whispers of winter are heard in the early morning air,
Motionless patterns form of yellow and red on trees so straight and so tall,
As the season patiently waits to move on its turn.

As the waters of the river start to freeze and autumn's race is run,
Gentle snowflakes fall in the fields, and winter's ice cold season looms,
As the trees are dusted by frost which glistens in the cool winter's sun,
And the earth once more sleeps, the red-breasted robin sings his tune.

Where has the winter gone, asks the snowdrop in the earth,
As ivy beneath green tinged hawthorn creeps,
And they raise their tiny heads to tell of spring's rebirth,
Bringing once more new beginnings and a sense of hope for you and me.

Gillian Sanbrooke

CONSERVATION

From the smallest of the small
To the biggest of the big
From the largest of the oak trees
To the shortest of the twigs.

I care for all the insects
And I tiptoe as I pass
To where all the furry animals live
In their homes amongst the grass.

If only we could see the danger
And open both our eyes
Then perhaps all the future children
Will see all the butterflies.

I worry for this planet
That we all call our home
And it's nice to know I'm positive
That in my thoughts, I'm not alone.

So if we can pull together
And stop building all the roads
And polluting all the water-ways
That's home to all the toads.

Conservation is important
No matter what the people say
For imagine what the world would be like
Without the things that make our day . . .

Brian Towner

THE MOUNTAIN

The mountain was a peaceful place
Wild flowers, some of which were rare,
Grew in abundance, smothering the rock face,
Forming a confused collage everywhere.

Skylarks nested. Rock pipits too.
In spring the gorse was alive with song.
Bright, bursting pods of yellow flew
Into the sky where swallows belong.

Undisturbed, sun-drenched adders would bask
Whilst lizards, stoats, shy foxes did roam.
Each intent on its tenuous task
To create a safe wildlife home.

Seven hundred feet above the stormy sea;
Safe from human predators,
Secret nature survived, pollution free.
Nourished by sun and windblown spores;

Flourished a luxuriant growth
Of uncultivated, wild, rain cleansed terrain;
Of its mysteries, ancient Druids spoke
Performing full moon rituals in vain.

White robed priests in oak groves
Disturbed dark unleashed power
From the mountain their evil flows
All its beauty man's greed will devour.

Wanton neglect as the heath fire blows.
Motorbikes roar through torn tranquillity;
Oblivious to the destruction they cause,
Helped by a Celtic council's hypocrisy;
In not upholding conservation laws.
The mountain now belongs to the motorbike and horse!

Jean Houghland

NELLIE

Wind that whistles through the trees,
Branches dip and sway,
Creatures scurry through the undergrowth
Taking cover, out of the way.
Typhoon Nellie whips the dust
Uproots the trees,
Everything is destroyed in her path.
People in the cellar sit and shiver
Waiting for the blast to pass.
A solitary moment whilst time stands still.

A prayer is said, and then once more into
The still air they crawl,
To survey all around.
A bird attempts a cheerful note whilst
Searching for her nest.
A lone dog crawls out of a hole
And tail between his legs
Makes tracks for home.

A baby cries, and now movement all around,
Each one a task to perform,
To salvage the few dusty remains,
A home to remake, a place to rest.
Nellie has passed.

Babs Morris

A FOREST WALK

A walk through the forest
Means time by myself
Though I'm never alone
For the lives on the ground
Above and below
Keeps my company when I'm out
On my own

The colours are changing
Each week of the year
There's beauty that always delights
And, as I walk through the seasons
I pause at a time
That for me is most wondrous of all

The life of the new
Blows freely around
All I see is once more awake
And as I gaze through the trees
At what lays ahead
I know the spell has truly been cast

A carpet of blue
Lays beneath all the trees
Like velvet its richness is pure
The bluebells display
All the magic of spring
Mother Nature has truly done well

Paula Stedman

PAINTED LADIES

Fragile butterflies - patterned wings,
Painted ladies - such pretty things!
As if coloured by a fairy hand
They travel from a far-off land
On so delicate a wing -
And, here, often to a thistle cling!
It is sad - they have become so rare -
Will they return? - For we should care -
One of *summer's* beauties - its life should not be extinct -
But, each season shows nature's compliment.

Mildred E Wood

ALDERSTEAD HEATH

Dew-gentle rain was falling
On the Surrey scene.
Late blackbird loud was calling
From a tree-top green.

The evening light was fading
Over the misty Down.
A pheasant was parading
Along a furrow brown.

A bluebell wood was glowing
With a purply hue.
A distant herd was lowing;
A cuckoo sang anew.

Heavy was the evening air
With the scented may.
Nothing could ever be more fair
Than that Surrey day.

Megan Hughes

FLIGHT TO RECOVERY

'You've strained your back!' the doctor said
 'Lie flat until it's better.'
My husband wasn't used to this
 but followed to the letter.
What a pain! What a plight!
'He's not sane!' 'Just not right!'

We put the bed downstairs
 and he could see the great big firry tree.
The birds were busy seeking space
 in which to raise a family.
Suddenly! Birds to spot!
He was free. Pain forgot.

So day by day his company
 the doves incessant cooing.
As happily the gentle bird sat near
 to do his wooing.
Sparrows pull - pampas plumes
Bird bath's full - starling zooms.

It's hard to spot the shy blue-tit
 who dips and darts collecting.
The robin stops his daily trill
 his wife and eggs protecting.
Twigs and leaves - magpie's beak
Pulls and heaves - hear that creak.

'Oh look! The baby sparrow's faces!
 peeping from the eaves!'
Excited husband full of pride in
 what each bird achieves,
Leaves his bed - try to fly
Enough said - so goodbye.

Marj Norton

NATURE'S WAY

Birds are singing in the trees
Their sweet notes floating on the breeze
Nests built high in swaying branches
The cuckoo calling out to tell us
Spring is here, with brighter days
Primroses and daffodils growing in nature's way.

The sun is warm, buds burst into flower
Shrubs and bushes glowing in glorious colour
Cherry blossom, so beautiful and the copper beach
Carpets of bluebells and fresh green leaf
A walk through the woods on a summer day
Where ferns and wild flowers grow, in nature's way.

Then comes the harvest of wheat and corn
Bales of new cut hay stacked in the barn
The earth is warm from the summer sun
Mellowed leaves on the trees turn to gold and brown
All the wonderful colours of the autumn days
We remember and remind us, of nature's ways.

The rain soaked leaves are on the ground
Wind stripped trees and hedges bare all around
Very cold and bleak the clouds are low
Birds have migrated away from the snow
Time for holly and mistletoe and for Christmas fir
It's nature's way of saying, winter is here.

Lorna June Burdon

THE WORLD ABOUT US

Nature is a wonderful thing and so is spring
The birds busy building their nests while they sing
Buds are beginning to peep through the soil, you can see them show
The trees start getting fresh leaves, it is a lovely sight for I know

It's nice to see the lambs in the fields with the ewes having them near
Some lambs are so very small and soon are bouncing around like the deer
All the animals are lovely, some are dangerous, some are cuddly too.
They are all put on this earth for a reason, it is nice to go to the zoo.

Squirrels in the parks picking up nuts then scampering up the trees
Some are very tame and take the nuts out of your hand, then I am pleased
Rabbits running about in the fields, jumping through the grass
Out in the country where you find all kind of birds, I remember when
I was a lass.

Valerie Horton

IVY AND THE OAK

Is it now an unwelcome embrace
That you would discard in haste
Had you, but the foresight to know
That such love would from such small
beginnings grow

But the seed once sown
Is too late to disown
Or was it indifference to the love of the
vine.

That now covers you and your trunk entwine
Thus it is a form of love that smothers
Unique to each and the exclusion of others
But both it does condemn
Love and life to death in the end.

Brian Norman

A DATE IN SPRING

My friend and I met late one night
At first he gave me quite a fright.
My birds were early risers, so had filled their breakfast tray,
This I always did, as it was prepared for the following day
The rustling sound I heard that night, made me turn around and stare
So went indoors to find my torch to search from here to there.
The beam of light shone brightly
On a body curled up in a ball
Its legs tucked underneath which seemed to be very small
I fed my little stranger, with cool water and a dish of meat
And hoped he would enjoy, his nightly supper treat
I named him Columbo, it seemed to fit him so right
My hedgehog no longer a stranger my dear friend of the night.
From May to November, we were as close as close can be,
Then it was time for hibernation, he no longer needed me.
So with tears in my eyes, I said my goodbyes
Me well, I can't wait till next spring.
When nature decrees that Columbo and I will commune
With the earth and the trees.

Margaret Rose Akeroyd

THE RAVEN

High above on stony crag, inky black he sits
Looking down on loch and field
What tasty morsel will reveal,
From tiny mouse to stillborn lamb
The raven eats whatever he can.

He feels no sorrow, nor pity or pain
Nor does he care if it's sunny or rain,
He flies through the mist with his mate at his wing
On this stony crag the raven is king.

Brian Stott

INSPIRED BY NATURE

Winter has been long, cold and austere
The ground is hard, frosty and bare
When suddenly appear snowdrops, delicate and white
Harbingers of a new life and future bright
Nature is wonderful in her determination
And who could not help feel a sense of elation
When viewing ground ravaged by fire
For which the prognosis has been dire
One suddenly sees the persistent shoots of new life
Bringing hope to a world of trouble and strife
When we are sad and heavy of heart
Like nature we must make a fresh start
And put forth our own tentative shoots
Nurture and tend them till they develop strong roots
For happiness, like flowers, will come again
And grow in life's sunshine and rain
Let Nature be your inspiration
When overcome by feelings of desolation
She never, ever, throws in the towel
So dig in your life with hope as the trowel.

Margaret Meagher

TO POLLY (MY CAT)

Silence. No sound, no breath
This once beating heart now motionless
Gone in your timeless sleep
A soul, one free spirit to roam the night.

I hear you cry sometimes
Do I imagine it?
I cannot believe, do not want to believe
That you are dead.

Buried in the garden
Sleeping under the flower bed
Soft and whispering shadows of winter leaves
Covering, caressing, soothing by your side.

The winds may howl their distant
And disturbing melodies
But you are safe, unharmed and free
My beautiful, lingering fragment of time.

Jenny Amery

HERALD OF SPRING

Below it begins to stir
New roots embark on their search,
Seeking important nutrients and water for life.
A small shoot sprouts from the mother bulb,
Pushing its way with untold strength;
Earth, stones move, making way
For the small white tip,
It finds the light it needs and greens.
Leaves begin to grow,
Over the coming weeks they fall back to earth.
A bud pushes its way between the leaves
Reaching out towards the sky.
It bends towards the sun,
The paper thin sheath unfolds
Exposing the flower-head.
Six overlapping petals
Open out into a star
And in the centre
The trumpet heralds spring is here.
Soon - the flower withers and dies,
The mother bulb reclaims
Its needs from the old for the new,
To begin again next year.

Ian Lyon

RAIN

Rain drops, drops of dew
Did a dinosaur first drink you?
Difficult to comprehend
The rain I'm watching now descend
Fell before a sound was heard
Uttered from a beast or bird.
Refreshing then a paradise,
A world of forest, sea and ice.
Sparkling, pure, crystal clear,
No longer that now I fear.
Countless times you've returned to earth
To satisfy man's growing thirst.
To recompense he pollutes
There are no dinosaur's to shoot.

Barbara Moore

TREES

Wooden wonders of our world
Living legends growing across many landscapes
trees standing like giants
tall and dignified
nature's gentlemen
branches climbing skywards
with an air of gentleness about them
trees home to many nesting birds
providers of food and shelter
big and strong
but with a heart of gold
let us learn to respect trees
man and nature living in harmony
so future generations can enjoy the beauty too
before trees are no more
that would be an unthinkable crime.

Neil Mason

CARESSING THE SENSES

Spectrum-hued reflections, shades,
Colour-lovely myriad forms:
From ocean depths, to arctic wastes;
Sunsets, flowers and the dawns,
The wonder of birds, a starry night;
Nature's beauty through sight.

Splashes, trickles, sea-surge boom,
Wind-rushed air, bird song aloft,
Creature-sounds and thunder's might;
Dew-damp, sand grain, petal soft
Breezes, thorn-prick and all such;
Nature through hearing, touch.

Sea-salted-lips taste, flavours-full,
Water spring-chilled, mulled wine;
Sun-warmed gorse and new-cut grass,
Wild primrose, lilac, pungent pine;
Memories stirred, emotions rent;
Nature tasted and through scent.

Caressing the senses, nature's beauty
Steals deep-down heart wise.
Filling the mind, God's gift
Of creation, uplifts and satisfies.

Maureen Sanders

SPRINGTIME

There's a song to be sung when the spring has begun
And the cold winter days near their end;
For the earth then breaks forth with the start of new birth
Which we welcome as a long lost friend.

From the slumber earth wakes and the days start to break
At an earlier dawn with much light.
And the birds start to sing with a bright cheery ring
As they gather and then they take flight.

Streams and rivers will flow, as on their way they go,
With fresh life at the end of the thaw.
The lambs gaily play in the fields every day
And there are chicks and rabbits galore!

The buds of the trees emerge from winter's freeze
And the daffodils and crocuses unite
To carpet the ground with colours to astound
And the green grass adds to the glorious sight.

For the true beauty of spring thanks to the Creator we'll sing -
To God who is seated on high;
For all His creation there is much elation
When the coming of springtime is nigh.

But we must not forget the most important thing yet
That this time of year to us brings.
To remember our Lord who stayed faithful to the Word
As he hung on the cross for our sins.

But Hallelujah we sing with the news Easter brings
That Jesus arose from the dead and He lives.
Eternal life for all who know Him as Saviour and Lord
And we give thanks for the true life He gives.

So our joyous song we will sing, at the turn of the spring,
That earth is awaking from winter's rest;
That our Lord Jesus lives and true hope he gives
For all - yes, springtime is best!

Martine L Shelton

THE LIVING PLANET

I have seen nature green and fertile
her flowery meadows, leafy trees.
I have seen nature blue and vital
her deep clear lakes and windswept seas.

I have seen nature red and fiery
bursting from a volcano's mouth.
I have seen nature white and frozen
her polar icebergs north and south.

I have seen nature hot and baking
her desert sands where little grows.
I have seen nature remote and lofty
her mountains clothed in perpetual snows.

I have seen nature strong and noisy
her jungles clamouring at the dawn.
I have seen nature calm and tranquil
her rippling plains of wheat and corn.

I have seen nature's many faces -
her beauty never fades away -
her boundless wealth of new experiences,
her ways mysterious still today.

Rowena Pollard

KINGFISHER

Silver dagger beak:
Fisherman's envy.
Robe of azure
And warm orange
Outdoes the latest
Paris fashions.

Naturally brilliant
The kingfisher watches
For his prey.
We watch him
Getting the attention
That some humans crave.

Samantha Jones

A SPRING WALK

I feel so special, though I cannot see
Why this special feeling should be in me!

But the sky above is a brilliant blue,
There are leafless trees where the blue shines through,
There are noiseless planes above me so high
Leaving their white tails criss-crossing the sky.
There are buds on the trees of palest green,
A musical chorus from birds unseen,
In verges beside me celandines grow,
While tractors hum in the fields below.
The dog from the farm nearby barks to say:
'I'm feeling fine on this wonderful day!'
When the lone car drones up the drumble track,
Then the sheep on the hillside answer back,

And the warm sun breathes on me.

Sheila E Harvey

NATURE

God created the world
So beautiful and pure,
Then blessed it with life forms
That we see as nature.
In this wonderful world
That is our planet earth
We are part of nature,
And give thanks for our birth.

Yet, still we despoil it
In our own foolish ways,
Polluting surroundings
With chemicals and sprays.
With nuclear power
And its radiation,
There is always the risk
Of a conflagration.

Nature may recover,
But we should take more care,
As one day, what is now
Will no longer be there.
Do not oppose nature,
Live close with it instead,
As, if we do not listen,
We shall soon all be dead.

Patricia Thomas

ALIVE AND KICKING

I love to hop and skip and shout,
and watch the daises coming out.
The baby lambs they are so white,
Will they be alright tonight?
When shadows fall and it gets cold
it can get chilly as we grow old.
I love to wake up with the birds
and listen to their song.
Isn't it wonderful how a great huge oak tree,
survives for so very long.
The fields of corn glow in the hazy sun,
as the farmer's get their work all done.
Spring turns to summer and summer to fall
I just can't decide which I like best of all.
The strong scent of blackberries
are a feast to my nose.
But actually it's winter, if I had to choose.
The holly bush glistens with berries so red
that they make joyful memories of Christmas
swirl around in my head.

Gaynor Davies

SILENCE

Silence isn't quiet;
there are noises all around.
Noises in the air and there
are noises on the ground.
Listening to silence
is what I like to do.
I listen to it every day
then listen the whole night
through.

Silence isn't everywhere.
It's only in certain places.
It's never in a rock song,
it's never at the races.
Find a suitable place
where silence is all around.
Where silence is in the air
and where silence is on the
ground.

Simon Harris (7)

MEADOW FLOWERS

Meadow flowers are
spirits of the wild;
marguerites in white star
patterns - shine
with buttercups - the field's reply
to sunbeams.
Cornflowers, mild
and shy
as secret dreams,
pale as the sky at twilight -
grow beside
proud poppies - tall
and radiantly bright -
that far and wide
display their
bold design -
in colours of warmth for all
the world to share.

Sylvia Cole

DAWN BESIDE LAKE WINDERMERE

Black topped reeds
channel into slimness against
          first puff of dawn
dark shadows
ruffle the bedspread of lakeside water.
Breezes
lift torpid ruffles into sharp edges
          of liquid brightness.
Uncertain haze
drifts lazily morningwards
blossoms yawn
lift sleep-heavy faces to slowly
          ripening sun

Morning thoughts turn gladly to a summer's day.

Peggy Netcott

TREE HEAL HEART

Stand in the middle of the blossoming tree
Amidst its pink clusters on heavy hanging bows -
Your whole head and body encompassed; engulfed inside
the pinkness.
You're in it - inside the space of the tree, experiencing it -
Soaking up its essence.
Feeling and smelling pink and cherries your whole world becomes
A place made of abundantly pink and heavenly scented blooms.
Just stay there, feel the soft petals brush your nose
Closed eyes and opened ears, feel your hair tangle up with
this forth giving tree.
Pink, pink, pink, the path you're going down is getting pinker and
Pinker, pinky pink, lovely and lovelier. Rosy love;
Loving heart, attached love. Care not duty.

Rachel Lott

TWILIGHT

As shadows fall across the tired earth
The evening sun lies bleeding in
the west
And birds upon the wing fly home
So swiftly to their nest
The flowers all their perfumed petals close
And meadows weep with glistening dew
The trees stand tall like ghosts and slowly sway
As twilight steals the end of day
Soon now the sky a different colour take
As night feels sorry for the earth below
A velvet blue drips diamonds like a crown
Behold the stars of night peer down
And moonbeams in a veil of lace
Fall softly on the earth's quiet face.

Christina

OUR ROBIN REDBREAST

When springtime arrives he pays us a visit
He chirps away heartily - or is it -
His way of asking for a wee bit to eat
A handful of crumbs or a wee bit o'meat.

He sits on the fence chirping away
And he never thinks about flying away
Until he has the crumbs we have on the tray
Then he flutters his wings and goes on his way
He'll be back tomorrow and each day for weeks
We'd be happy if we had him for keeps
But the day will come when he makes up his mind
To leave us at present until next springtime.

S T Jennings

SPRINGTIME

I walk through the fields
There I see the colours she yields
In the spring the flowers bloom
To wash away the winter's gloom
How I love the spring
The trees get new leaves
They reach up higher
Like to touch the sky is their desire
The sun in the morning
Creeps in when we're yawning
Like a fire of golden red
It lights the world
All the flowers then become uncurled
Into this, our beautiful world
How I love the spring
The birth of animal cubs
The marking of new life
It's a time when worry and strife
They're out of my life
I just sit and watch the show
Watch the animals and flowers grow
I let the sun tickle my face
Each ray like fingers
The warmth and the beauty
How I love the spring.

C Harris

THE WORLD ABOUT US

After snow in January
The snowdrops show their heads
In February crocuses
Grow gently in their beds.
March brings winds
And April showers
Spring daffodils appear,
May and June are halfway
Through the year
Roses are now appearing
Summer is on the way
It's nature's way of saying
The sun is here to stay.
Isn't Nature wonderful
It rejuvenates us all
If only time could pause awhile
We'd enjoy it, most of all.
July, August, September
Autumn is on the way
Bringing us the falling leaves
And shortening our day.
October and November
Bring us fog and skies of grey,
But they only make a way
For Xmas in December.
We greet our friends anew
What a wonderful world
We live in,
A world so shiny and new.

Win Davies

THE WORLD ABOUT US

This world is still full of wonder, everywhere you go
The beauty of nature, new life growing with each plant you sow.
In the sky there is the sun by day to give us light
And the moon and twinkly stars, to brighten us each night.
There's the mountains, hills, valley's and the dells
And forests, orchards and farms, where often cattle dwell
Oceans, waterfalls, lakes, rivers and the seas with waves high and low
Often there is rain, hail, snow that falls to help all things to grow
God created everything and gave it to us all to share you know.
We are human beings, maybe white or coloured, rich or poor
Each has human nature and one must open their own door
But today many are demanding they must have more and more
They use hate, violence and even murder leaving old folks
Lying dead upon the floor. It's time more human nature found
Time to send to God a prayer. To thank Him for all He gave us, and all
His love and care, and please God we ask You for help, strength
Courage, we have troubles hard to bear. Dear Lord this is our prayer
That in 'The World About Us' we'll try together to make living
For everyone to be much more loving, but it must be fair.

Gertie Boxall

MARCH MEDITATION

The breeze that spun the spent leaves down
Now speeds the snowdrop on its way;
The wind that swirled the blizzard by
Laughs with the daffodils today.

Now violets breathe their sweetness where
November's sodden flotsam fell;
And crocus flambeaux blaze abroad,
News of the stirring year to tell.

Swifter than light, summer slips by,
        Again the golden leaves will fall.
Again the earth will cringe in ice,
        And slumber in a snowy pall.

But as we mourn the dying years
        Shrouded in grey and darkening skies,
We can look on, as now, and know
        March sunshine warms June's butterflies.

Margaret Andrews

SEASONS

In every season of the year,
Something can be found to cheer.
We only have to look around,
For all God's wonders can be found.

In springtime shoots begin to show,
The daffodils sway to and fro.
Baby lambs all skip and bleat,
The air is chilly the sun a treat.

In summer we have happy days,
Our pleasure found in many ways.
The flowers bloom in bright array,
Sea and sand, sunshine to stay.

In autumn we get wind and rain,
The colourful leaves that carpet our lane.
Shiny brown conkers we find on the ground,
The harvest all in, much fruit to be found.

In winter the frost with an icy cold glow,
The snow falling softly, a snowman for show.
Warm fires and our slippers, armchair and a book,
And many more wonders, we just have to look.

Jill Pettitt

SEASONS OF THE YEAR

Summer. autumn, winter, spring
the four seasons of the year
Summer - the hottest time of all
when the sun is shining
down on us all.
Autumn - is cool and crisp like
nice for going for walks
when leaves are falling
to the ground,
Winter - the coldest time of all
when snow is all around
and icy- slippery roads
Spring - the best season of all
with everything fresh and new
which is your best season?
Summer, autumn, winter or spring?

Linda Casey

APRIL VIOLETS

A flower growing under a canopy of green,
Its tiny purple petals barely seen,
But its fragrance is heaven made,
Until its blossoms gradually fade,
Its scent, however, is captured for our pleasure,
With many happy memories to treasure
Of wooded glades in spring,
Trilling small birds on the wing,
The call of the cuckoo flying by
The singing of the lark high in the sky,
Sweet April violets, your scent lingers on,
When more exotic perfumes have gone.

Ivy Louise Wright

MY RAINBOW FROM HEAVEN

I love walking in the rain
Feeling the dampness on my hair
Watching children playing in the puddles
Smelling the sweetness in the air

But when the storm clouds gather
And the sky darkens for a squall
I can feel my heartbeat quicken
I don't like thunderstorms at all.

The winds rage, the thunder roars
I run swiftly home to hide
When it claps outside my window
I thank God I'm safe inside.

Then a flash of lightning strikes
Like a rocket across the sky
I peek from behind the curtain
It's so frightening I could cry.

So I huddle in the corner
With my face hidden in my hands
I put my fingers in my ears
To banish sights and sounds.

When the storm at last is over
And the clouds slowly disappear
With the first ray of sunshine
Easing through, I overcome my fear

I look up to the heavens
And there for all to see
Is a coloured spectrum in the sky
A rainbow, just for me.

Christina R Maggs

MODERN REVERDIE

Sweetly walks my love
Early summer joy
Laden Sussex lanes
Smell of hawthorn blossom
Aroma of cancer.

Oi my lover
Lady lout, yah-boo snob,
Reckon yourself a cut above
After a hundred summers fade,
You will be as dead as me.

Sweetly rots my love
Japanese knotweed creeps
Carrion crows sing
Smell of hawthorn blossom
Aroma of cancer

Martin Vine

SPRING

See the bluebells dancing in the month of May
And the cuckoos calling, what a lovely day.
All around is sunshine, rippling through the trees,
And the scent of bluebells carried on the breeze.
Birds are busy nesting, flying to and fro,
People in their gardens busy with a hoe.
You must guess it's springtime, Britain at its best,
Filling all God's creatures with energy and zest.

A P Stevens

ONCE MORE WITH FEELING

The mayfly bonks itself senseless because
Its life lasts for only one day:
But with people it can take a while to get started
Until things start to warm up in May.

The pansies come out, the daffodils bloom
And the skimpies all start sliding down;
Because spring's in the air and things stand up proud
As naked white turns slowly brown.

People start smiling and saying 'hello'
Looking forward to weekends with reason;
They can't wait to jostle, to argue and haggle,
It's the start of the boot-sale season.

The beaches are packed and there's nowhere to park,
En' mass sunburn, sucking fast melting ices;
Deck chairs are lurid against fish belly white,
And cold drinks reach ridiculous prices.

White plastic tables sneak out of the shed,
Burgers 'n' bangers become barbecues;
Dad brings his old baggy shorts out to play,
With his embarrassing brown Jesus shoes.

In the parks thighs are spreading and bottoms are bouncing,
Love imprints are left in the ground;
As once more, with feeling we come round to spring,
On the nature trail merry go round.

Steve Sutton

THE SEASONS COME AND GO

The spring comes and the flower buds and plants start to appear
Without a sound they grow so tall and silently
As they come through with the warms of the summer's sun
The beautiful flowers and the vegetables and
crops in the field ready for the yield
Then they just disappear into the ground without a sound.
As the autumn comes in and the sound of
rustling leaves as they fall to the ground.
As the glistening frost is everywhere as
the trees become so bare
The winter starts to come in as the snow starts to cover the ground
So white so pure as the start of the coming new year
Then a miracle happens as you see buds around
You know spring has come as the snow melts away
For on this earth every day is a perfect day
As life goes on in this wonderful way

M B Thorpe

BEAUTIFUL BUTTERFLY

They meet at the bottom of gardens
Where tall lovely lollipops grow
As you flit along from flower to flower
You enchant me every minute and hour.

Where a pink fairy swings
On a butterfly's wing
We know summer is here when we see you around
You spread out your wings and prepare to fly.

We gaze in wonder as you pass by
The marvels of nature is all there to see
The lovely colours on your wings
Butterfly, butterfly, you bring so much pleasure.

Heather Aspinall

THE WORLD ABOUT US

You feel blue - no, not you,
You should like the lambs be prancing
In the lush green field a'dancing,
For it's spring you know.

Out in your garden you should be
Seeking, searching especially
For tiny shoots, and buds so green
Peeping shyly on the garden scene.

Each day brings another form
Beauty in flower, or tree with thorn,
Every type of bud or stem
Reveals another priceless gem.

They've laid down low up until now
Under the rich brown earth I vow
Has kept them alive while they slept
Whilst a few of them have faded and wept.

Everything's moving and growing up fast,
Beautiful colours in flowers that last
To brighten the gardens for all to see
With the gentle breeze blowing them free.

Daffodils yellow grow stately and tall
Amidst their friends so cute and small,
The birds are in song from far and near
Twittering in trees for spring is here.

Still feeling blue - no, not you
You've been down to the garden today.
Go again tomorrow, and you will find
That God has remembered all mankind
For spring is here.

Evelyn Goldsmith

THE WAY OF THINGS

As nature shakes her head from sleep; unlocking
the frozen earth to spring, and the snowdrops'
slender grace hides deep within a sheltered
place, the fields have cast off winter dress
to wear spring's opulent loveliness; and as the
woods let go of secret things, velvet deer, the
song of hurrying wings, I come across a babbling
brook where tall trees with sunlight in their
hair stand among the flowers fair, and as I
wander down roads and stony lanes; the wind
laughs low with tender breezes and my eye beholds
my heart's desire, woods and dales; primrose pale,
the fields and fields of daffodils, and as I walk
towards my gate upon the ripping tide of night;
I think of tomorrow yet to come, when God's
overcoat is yet again undone, and as nature takes
its course I will see the beauty of another day;
soaring me to fields of joy.

Martinella Brooks

NATURE'S PURE HANDS

(Ode to my Great-Gran, Eileen Camps)

Cold eroded cliffs,
warm in the breeze
their stones hold many mysteries.

Force of the sea,
shore's secret sands
forgotten footsteps shape this land.

Tears of generations
touch the ebbing tide,
granite hands of passion and pride.

The kiss of the cowslip,
caress of the corn
wheat whispers in the dusty dawn.

World's evolution,
in nature's pure hands
Earth's older than any man.

Eily Tatlow

LONG LIKE A SKYSCRAPER

An evergreen cotoneaster hedge,
Startlingly, nearly shorn of leaves
After a bitter-harsh winter.
In it - a nest, built like a skyscraper.
Four blue-tinged eggs, cuddled together.
Wary blackbirds hop, chattering.
I am too close.

Hatched on a dawn glowing with humid sun, warmly snug,
Tiny, lopsided bundles of skin.

My few days' vigil wonders at the shrewd secrecy of the parent
birds to nurture the young unseen.
Peep in carefully.
Four finger-nail sized babies, scraggy, lie piled, rotted together.

Were they reached by the unexpected hard frost the day after their
birth - met so soon by the reality of the world?
Or did I, by my simple curiosity, fright the mother bird away and
deal the killing blow?

Kathleen Wisely

THE NATURE POEM

When I was ten the teacher said
'A nature poem will be read
But first I want you to go home
And write a poem of your own.'
I had no trouble writing mine
It was complete by supper time.
My parents said it must be read
To them, before I went to bed.
The first two lines I read aloud
To them, and felt so very proud.

'Through the country lanes I love to roam
Where the ford makes a noise with its bubble and foam -'

Mother laughed and thought it funny
Father too, 'til his eyes went runny
Even neighbours laughed and laughed
And I the poet felt so daft.
Why should nature cause such fun?
Yes, I was the puzzled one!
'What's so funny Dad?' I said,
Now my poem had been read
'The bit about the ford,' he cried
'The bubble and foam that you described
It happened to our car today
And you were right in every way!'

Anne Beer

COUNTRY LIFE

Take my hand and come with me
To that old belovèd tree,
Along the winding footpath worn
By people over years were born.
By the brook forever babbling,
Endless in its ways of travelling,
Past the barley fields once more,
Where the field mice do explore.
Over the moles' hills always there,
On we'd go, why should we care,
See the old windmill still turning,
On the hills the corn stalks burning.
Cows at their trough having a drink,
Jackdaws on wires stopping to think,
Rabbits and hares in the hedges are playing,
The shaggy old sheepdog in the sun is laying.
The life in the country is always there
For people who bother to stop and stare.
The barns are all full, the haystacks are growing,
Fields ploughed up for next year's sowing,
The calves are all born for another season,
The cock is still crowing but now for no reason.
A kestrel hawk, hovering low,
Run all you little folk, run from your foe
To a country lover on a very still day,
The noise is incessant in every way.

Pauline Jackson

THE INVITATION

Away in the country out for a ride,
A shady glade my husband espied,
Come bide with me, just for a while,
Its message simple, without guile.

The invitation was gratefully accepted,
A favourite position carefully selected,
'Twas then I chanced to glance around
And saw the rubbish on the ground.

How sad, I thought, in utter dismay,
To see nature's green carpet spoilt in this way.
I closed my eyes to imagine the scene,
Saw this beautiful place as it could have been,
A lovely spot in which to roam,
With all the litter taken home.

Audrey K Price

OBSERVATION

Just an ordinary moth at the window pane,
Intent on the usual orgy of self-destruction:
To be singed to death by the heat of the electric orb.
The sudden, reflected glint of an amber eye
Attracted me - drew me to closer scrutiny.
Amazingly I saw a furry, oyster-shaded body;
Creamy wings, delicate as a veil of mist;
Eyes of topaz which burned with an inner fire;
Feelers as fine as cobweb tendrils.
Exquisite perfection in every God-given detail -
Just an ordinary moth at the window pane.

Julie Creaven

FOUR SEASONS' MAIDENS

She pursed her lips blowing gently down
And the pine trees softly swayed -
And they felt the caress of her balmy breath
O'er the land on that fine June day -
And they knew she was here -
That old friend they held dear -
The warming summer maid

When the autumn maiden spread her cloak -
The days grew short and cold -
As she blocked out the sun -
Cooler days had begun -
And the leaves became bronze and gold

With talons of icicles - sequins of snow -
The cold winter maiden we would soon know -
She'd cover the landscape white near and far -
In her shiny black hair -
Twinkling bright frosty stars -

As we sensed brighter days
With her smile she'd erase
Winter's grip - the spring maiden took hold
With her lyrical flute -
We would see the first shoot -
When bird song and blossom unfold

To the world they bring order -
They work unperturbed -
If four seasons' maidens
Are never disturbed

Dennis Curley

SEASONS

The year begins with snow and ice
Winter sun glistening on frost looks nice
Then it thaws and turns to rain
Nature stirs and it's spring again

The days lengthen and get lighter
The countryside looks much brighter
Birds build nests in hedges and trees
The winter winds turn into a breeze

Then it's the time when lambs are born
Blossoms and flowers the gardens adorn
Spring moves into summer once more
With lovely warm days the children adore

We spend time in the country or by the sea
For it's holiday time from work we are free
The fruit in the orchards begins to mellow
While the leaves on the trees change to yellow

Quickly it seems they turn gold and brown
And with autumn winds come floating down
Making a beautiful carpet under our feet
Trampling through them for me is a treat

Then foggy days are with us in November
Followed by long dark nights of December
The days are usually cold and grey
But everyone looks forward to Christmas Day

The sun has lost any warmth it had
But for all nature's changes we must be glad
The seasons' cycle takes just a year
So we must treasure them all and hold them dear.

Shirley Travis

NATURAL FORCES

(Romans 1 v 20)

Natural forces keep us alive
We more than survive, we thrive.
For in these forces God reigns at will
Showing to us His amazing skill.
A freelance artist with skills to spare
Designed with flair with the greatest care.
These forces at work are quiet and subdued
Having ramifications with exactitude.
Showing another skill of engineer
Replenishing itself year after year.
The creation's glory speaks alone
For more discovery we wait to be shown.
Invisible qualities clearly seen
To show us where brilliance has been.
From these forces there is no speech
Yet look at the beauty of the golden beech.
Beseeching us to take a closer look
At wide open oceans and the babbling brook.
To see the sunset slide down in red
And upon this earth place our feet to tread.
The natural forces are there to stay
Yet how do we know we'll get through today.

Denise Shaw

GROWING

The baby birds trapped in their eggs,
Hitting the sides furiously.
Then at last they break free
Waiting for the worms for their dinner.

Benjamin Monk (8)

THE PRINCES IN THE TOWER

The year is fourteen eighty-three
The day - Midsummer's Day
As I gaze from a window in the Tower
On London, bright and gay.

Just weeks ago, this London
Held subjects, true and loyal
To me Edward, their king,
And brother Richard, royal.

God save our brave young King
In unison they cried
Now their lips are silent
Their cries and cheers have died.

Once rightful heirs to a nation
True sons of merry England
Now our youth is locked away
For ever gone our kingdom.

The sun in splendour has eclipsed
A shadow hides its rays
Now Uncle Gloucester holds the crown
And takes away our days.

Darkness into the chambers creeps
As I lay and sleep and dream
Of haunting blood-stained spectres
And try hard not to scream

An angel floats in mid air
Two crowns above her head
Are they the crowns of King and York?
Are we soon to join the dead?

Footsteps on the turret stairs
The creak of the chamber door
Voices whispering, shadows looming
A rustling through the straw
On Midsummer's night in London town

Two tortured souls fly free
Gone are the Princes in the Tower
In this year of fourteen eighty-three.

Terence Raymond

A PICTURE OF SPRING

The days of winter, dark and long,
Icy cold . . . almost gone,
As summer signs begin to show . . .
. . . Green buds popping, as they grow.

Blackbirds busy . . . from crack of dawn,
Making homes for their newborn.
Pastel colours everywhere . . .
. . . Not a hedgerow is left bare.
Snowdrops dancing in the breeze . . .
. . . Carpets of white . . . beneath the trees.

Forget-me-nots, violets too . . .
. . . Blend together with shades of blue.
Primroses and the celandine peep through the grass . . .
. . . When the sun starts to shine.

This glorious rebirth never ceases to amaze . . .
. . . Each year, these beautiful springtime days.
Mother Nature works hard for us,
Painting these pictures, without a fuss.

It's up to us humans too,
To respect her work in all that we do,
Tread carefully . . . do not mar
This springtime masterpiece,
The best picture by far.

Pat Drew

THE HILL

The Hill is ours
We live on and around it
We are the Hill's people. Since time began
Our forebears lived on it and around it
In little clusters of shelters, they and their beasts.
Each little cluster becoming, in time a village,
A village with its farms, its farm animals, its own manor,
The big house with its benevolence, its caring
For the people and homes around the hill.
Each village with its church built lovingly
By our stone cutting forebears, the craftsmen in the Hill's early life.
We, the newest people still see and love their carvings,
Their sturdy pillars whose strength still holds.
The intricate carvings, their beauty and wit still with us.
The Hill, which is so nearly a mountain, has seen it all.
Has seen, in its closely wooded early days, the feuds, the fights so bitter,
Swift arrows, pikes and swords fiercely defending its place.
Strangers to the island from over the water, so sure,
But beaten back from their camps by the Hill's own people.
The Hill has never been captured, never defeated.
Changed perhaps, great trees long gone,
But still our own, our roots embedded in its depths.
We defend it as fiercely as the early people
Against new enemies, more subtle, more insidious, more dangerous
But its people still strong and determined, fight,
And will go on fighting, the Hill and its people stand together.

Patricia Cobb

ICICLES

Red ball of sun
High in the winter sky
Snowflakes fall in between
Bright sunlight in my eye
Heavy cloud comes with icy cold air
January brings some people despair
Not for me though
I can see its winter glow
Brings its own kind of magic
The ice and the snow
Black trees red berries
Icy tips on lots of hedges
Silver crystals hanging down
Icy ponds would make no sound
With tiny prints frozen in the ground
To capture the moment of the day
Till the sun sets and leaves
This wonderful bright aurae

Patricia Flynn

SPRING

Brown scarred landscapes of death,
In a glimmer of weak sunlight,
Provide a barren canvas,
For splashes of colour.

Like a magician, pulling from his hat,
The earth bursts forth with
Greens, blue, yellow,
Colour of every hue.

Lorraine Sheldrake

NATURE'S OPEN WINDOW

As I walk along the footpaths towards the hill
Whilst taking in the air that is soft and still,
Birds acquaint me with their singing;
Distant church bells faintly ringing;
Blueflies dart and hum on by;
And nature opens up her window to my ever-watchful eye . . .

Cast in shadow - wild flowers beneath protective trees;
While grasses reach and bend and sprout and catch the slightest breeze.
The hedgerows shelter from the sun such tiny creatures that should come
And make their homes within the holds of twisted arms and leafy folds.
And in the hollow on the hill nature's night-life sleeps on still;
Yet their presence is quickly spied by the ever-conscious curious eyed -
Here a badger's sett; there a fox's lair;
And rabbit's fur and horse's hair;
And remnants of trees scattered at ground;
And fishes in streams darting around;
Bobbin' twigs and floating leaves -
Boats for fairies to retrieve . . .
Yet, I'm lost in thoughts in this peaceful hum -
Paradise for me *has surely* come . . .

Mary Pauline Winter

NEW BORNS

New born baby, calf or lamb,
Their lives are just beginning.
They will need all the help they can,
To get through life and winning.

In this world of ours today,
Where cruelty and lust abound,
These little mites depend on us,
We must not let them down.

Margarita Reeve

PARADISE LOST - A SUMMER MEMORY

I remember this special place near to our home,
where, as children, we played for many happy hours.
It seemed so grand as every inch we would roam,
carpeted in colour, a mass of wild flowers.
Often buttercups under our chins we would hold,
to see if we liked butter - they shone like pure gold.

Red and yellow poppies seemed to dance in the sun,
Whilst tall, proud grasses swayed gently in that fresh air,
as if trying to join in as we had our fun.
Nothing to worry us then, we hadn't a care,
for it seemed that all summers long we there would spend.
Happy together, the wildlife, me and my friend.

Tiny pink cuckoo flowers all covered in spit.
Violets peeping shyly along the hedgerow.
From flower to flower the honey bees would flit.
Birds singing merrily, their happiness to show.
It seemed like paradise, there, in our special field,
that forever its memory in our hearts is sealed.

Sadly, years on, we returned to find to our strife,
that our field had been ploughed up - no longer a sound.
For gone were hedgerows, flowers and all the wildlife.
Nothing! Just dirty brown earth to cover the ground.
Eyes shut tight, once more we beheld that well-loved sight,
Its blue sky marbled by clouds, all feathered in white.

It's tragic, future generations will not see
Nature as we did, its splendid diversity.
We were lucky, to run, laughing, shouting with glee
as we marvelled at each new discovery.
White daisies nestled lovingly around our feet,
they may only be left with a field of red beet!

Sheila Collins

ROSE

As my gaze falls on pink rosebuds
I see the promise of new life.
The tight bud is like the baby,
Cerise and covered in creases.
Just waiting to burst forth and bloom,
And enrich us with its presence.
Proudly peeking through pink petals
The young rose naively blossoms.
Resplendent in ruddy raiments
And flushed with eager enthusiasm,
The rose stretches its tips skywards
And its life begins to unfold.

Once open, the rose radiates life.
Blush petals like soft sensuous skin
Inviting delicate caresses.
Hypnotic perfumes dreamily
Draw desirers to discover
Her innermost beauty within.
A most youthful, vibrant temptress
The blooming, voluptuous rose,
With arms outstretched in a welcome,
Entices endless paramours,
Enveloped by her rich bouquet,
To her soft scented sanctuary.

All too soon the summer will fade
And her rich beauty begins to ebb.
Pink petals lose their glow of youth
And pungent scent melts to a mist.
The odour gone, ardour follows.
Sensual softness slips away
To be replaced by ripe roughness.

Head bows, petals sag, body droops,
As age brings its own destiny.
The rose is cut down and burnt
And the ashes sprinkled in the ground
To allow life to be renewed.

Peta C C Vale

THE CHANGING SEASONS

Spring
The sunshine stretches into action,
Thawing my bones with a stroke so warm,
All of nature seems to catch on,
And the early birds chorus the dawn.

Summer
Shimmering heat envelopes me,
Winged insects jostle for air space,
Flowers in bloom boast their beauty,
A breath of breeze holds me in embrace.

Autumn
Misty mornings hail the change,
Spiders spin webs of lace and dew,
Shivers arrive as the harvest moon wanes,
Trees shed crisp leaves of every hue.

Winter
The wretched wind claws at my clothes,
Sleet and hailstones lash my skin,
Numbness grasps at fingers and toes,
My body surrenders and winter wins.

Sarah J Lane

ON THE SOCIAL ORGANISATION OF STING NETTLES

In a bank of sting nettles
There is always one that is tallest,
The king nettle,
Or queen nettle, I don't know which;
If you cut down
Or dig up those round the edges
It doesn't matter to the others,
But if you kill the top nettle
The rest lose heart,
Are badly set back.
Like ants, bees and wasps, nettles
Are social beings.
Nettles hold no elections,
I do not know if they have
An hereditary
Principle. But some time
After top nettle has gone
A successor emerges.

Jean Overton Fuller

SUMMER'S WOE

I'm Mother Nature's rebel son
whose summer charms I'd rather shun,
whose grains of life to me are death,
that leave me blind and short of breath.
I find the heat that brings forth fruit
a spiteful, unrelenting brute,
and cower from the cosmic gun,
whilst others burn themselves for fun.

So give me winter's frosty bite,
the kind and everlasting night
when nature's dance is done.

Malcolm Brown

A WALK IN THE WOODLAND

The skies are blue, and the grass a brilliant green,
The birds fly so high above; almost unseen,
The woodlands flourish, with fruits they do bear,
For the small, wonderful creatures which choose to bide there,
The little lake glistens in the mid-morning sun,
Giving refreshment to all, each and every one,
The flowers they dance, and sway with the breeze,
As they spread round their seeds with the greatest of ease,
The swift, darting dragonflies which rush here and there,
Fly round the forest with not one single care,
The rabbits and foxes play, youthfully, through the day,
The birds, how they chatter, but not much do they say,
The wind gently whistles as it dances around,
The squirrels gather fruits which lay on the ground,
The trees grow so tall almost reaching the sky,
Providing shelter and food for all who pass by,
Mother Nature worked hard at this glorious place,
To make a safe haven and keep her creatures safe,
She created many sights for us to see when we pass by,
She made many sounds and fresh smells to tantalise,
I hope far off in the future Man leaves well alone,
And not disturb this beauty spot; which to many is a home,
It's a wonderful place and long may it stay,
Just passing by in the morning - brightens the day.

Tracey Thomson

SPRINGTIME IN BELLINGHAM

Early this morning
I opened the door
and walked out, to inhale
the fragrance
of a fresh spring day.

Something was happening . . .
I could feel it in the air,
and sensed movement
under the winter sod.

Life was emerging
from the ground, uncurling
tight fists of energy,
to spread green fingers of foliage
across the bare brown earth.

Sap flowed once more
through the once stiff branches
of the wintry woodlands.

The air was pulsating . . .
a breathing and a heaving
All nature in travail
to bring forth the gift of spring.

Daffodils erect - blowing
their yellow trumpets
across the chill March winds.

Birds calling for their mates
sing songs so sweet,
that ears hold still in wonder.

Rosemary Scott

THE DAWN OF SPRING

The winter has been harsh and long,
With cloudy skies and snow and rain.
We thought we'd never hear the song
Of birds, or see the sun again.
Below the hard and frozen earth
The seeds lay dormant in the ground,
Waiting for that miracle,
When once again the spring comes round.

Then buds appear on all the trees,
And gardens bloom in white and gold.
With daffodils and crocuses,
Shy violets and tulips bold.
Blue skies above do cheer us all
As everything begins to grow.
Green fields and blossoms everywhere,
As nature gives her yearly show.

And so it is within our lives,
When days are dark and full of pain.
We feel that winter's here to stay,
And tears keep falling like the rain.
Until one day a friendly smile
Or kindly word comes shining through,
Then in our hearts it's spring again,
And life starts blossoming anew.

Enid Crowhurst

LISTEN TO THE TREES

A summer's day with gentle breeze.
Just listen and you will hear the trees
They talk amongst themselves you see
So listen and you will hear the trees.
This is what I heard them say
When I was listening one summer's day.
It was a mighty oak who first shook and then spoke
'I am the biggest and the best'
To which a cedar replied
'I'm older than you and all the rest.'
'Did you see that person shelter under me'
Shouted a large spreading horse chestnut tree.
'Have you seen my catkins, aren't they fine?'
Said a tearful willow to a towering pine.
'I think that I'm the most elegant here'
Shrieked a snooty elm with a nasty sneer.
'I disagree I think that's me'
Said a tall and upright poplar tree.
'What silly things you all have to say
I am used for cooking, because I am a bay.'
'Well I'm most important, just feel my wood.
I bet you would all like to be beech if you could.'
Suddenly the breeze increased and started to grow stronger.
It got chilly and I could not stay to listen any longer.
But as I stood up from beneath a large tree
I'm sure I heard it talking about me.

Marilyn Warne

PRICELESS THOUGHTS

Winds blow the notes to dance in the breeze.
Branches they bounce in time on the trees.
While high on the top of the bird sings its tune.
Nature is lovely in the month of June.

I lay my soul to rest in the sun.
A deep breath of air, contentment's begun.
The fragrant smell of flowers drift by
Like perfumed air on the grass as I lie.

Oh what a creation we have and don't know,
Absorbing the feeling from life as we grow.
Each thing in its beauty like diamond's the stone,
Taken for granted, our everlasting home.

The earth is the home for billions to see
Reproductions of everything from land to the sea.
From rocks to the mountains, soil, sand and stream,
There's people and animals and things that are unseen.

The world is a wonder when time for some thought.
Shapes with their colours precise as it ought.
Each country is different and know by its name,
And yet not so different, just repeated again.

Freedom enjoyed to see, hear and smell.
I glance at my watch, the time to tell.
I rise to my feet contented with thought.
It is grand no price to be bought.

Delline Docherty

THE ROSE

Earth has brought to life a daughter.
She is of glorious beauty untold.
She has a head of promising colour,
And a grace of divine goodness.
Wearing a dress of green frills to thrill,
Sharp spikes to fright,
They travel down her elegant body,
A body of passion and tenderness,
And a love to behold forever.
There is nothing held so dear
As the beauty of this our rose,
Brought to us by the magic
Of nature's hidden secrets.

Carol Gilby

TO BLUEBELLS

In May you came, a brilliant blue,
later than you usually do.
I welcomed you with open arms,
quite besotted with your charms.
At that time there were few of you

but then you grew and grew and grew,
took over lawn and pathways, too.
Friends enthused, but I had qualms
(in May)

for I knew what labours would ensue
when I dealt with your bells as I have to do.
Each year when you come in massive swarms
my attitude to *winter* warms!
My aching back and arms I rue
in May.

Geraldine Squires

SPRING

Winter flies away at last,
As life cocoons the recent past.
The colour change announces spring
With panoramic scenes to bring;
The hedgerows, violets, coltsfoot flower
That bursts in bloom, proclaiming power.
A vivid, yellow, primrose hue
Enshrouds the grass, divides the dew.

Iridescent blues and mauves
Reflect the plumaged birds aloft
Where weeping willows hang their heads
With branches clothed in catkins' spread.
The cherry trees display pink light
As fragile petals gather flight.
When seas of apple blossom spark
The sleeping beds, where loved ones' marks
Are etched on stone for all to see,
Their spirit like the spring is free.

Regeneration fills the air
Awakening re-established flair,
With luscious dreams of mortal span
Conducting style, reviving man.
No matter how our lives revolve
For spring will heal and then resolve
To knit the pattern closely sewn
Which Mother Earth gives out on loan.
For man and beast to state their case
And weave the web of binding lace,
Which ties the bricks of life itself
Encasing all their worldly wealth.

Josephine Duthie

WATER OF DREAMS

Nestling between the steep banks
the busy stream threaded its way,
protected by guardian trees.
The bright afternoon sun glinted
on water, ruffled by eddies
as it poured, swirling round smooth stones.
Dark, overhanging banks made smoother
by thick moss, green and inviting.
Clear bubbles chased dreams as they went
on journeys of discovery.
Lying on the scorched grass, left behind
by last year's sun, a torn egg
from a blackbird gazed up, empty.
Not warmed by loving breast feathers
in a cosy nest. A victim,
not of hatching, but of thieving.
My sorrow salved by the balm of
musical water gurgling on
its way. Passing down to the sea.

Elizabeth Goffin

WINTER SUNSET

Skeletal alone it stands
Symbol of life's transiency,
Boughs outstretched like withered hands,
Glorious in its symmetry.
Black streaked with orange, shards of white -
The backcloth to approaching night.

A winter's sunset wild and raw -
Yet beautiful beyond delight;
The changing spread of colours draw
Such fantasies of dark and light.
Nature's palette black and gold,
Orange, grey and green behold.

The lowering clouds seem edged with fire,
A brook reflects the glow,
And all the elements aspire
To join like chariots of fire
And streak the earth below.

Eileen Reece

THE LOMONDS

Above Falkland,
A fleeting glimpse of
Mother Nature in her
Heavenly,
Amethyst negligee
Revealed her oriental breast,
White,
Firm and
Conical,
Contrasting markedly
With the occidental,
Severed
By Nature's surgeon,
Swathed in misty gauze,
Mimicking a mastectomy.

Suddenly,
Suspicious
Of my awe-struck gaze
She quickly concealed all
Under a mussel-blue sheet.

Jenny Burt

SPRING

Spring is here and new life is about to start.
The dark and wet nights are gone and so depart.
I see a young bird on the wing,
inspecting his new wings and trying to sing.
The little lambs running, springing and on the hop,
from early morn till dusk, not knowing when to stop,
New leaves on the trees tightly rolled up,
opening slowly and gracefully, daffodils like golden cups.
The grass starts to look like a green carpet again,
after a cold winter of snow and hard rain.
The plants are looking fresh and ready to bud,
I think I shall buy some new bulbs for the old green tub.
Just where do I start? There's so much to do.
I had a rest during the winter, oh the months just flew.
Now it's outside and many a chore,
But it's a garden I cherish, one I adore.
Oh such colour, changing by the day,
I said it would be hard work, but one day it would pay.
It's a joy to sit and watch as nature puts on a show,
Feel the sun on my face and end the evening with a glow.
As I lie in bed and the stars come out tonight,
I think tomorrow I shall grasp the spring and hold it tight.

Caroline Gill

OUR FOUR SEASONS

Spring it makes you bounce with joy,
The children do play out with their Christmas toy.
No buds on the trees and no bulbs will grow,
Now it's a bit warmer it just might snow.

A nice crisp morning for the sun to shine,
Things start to feel warm in the springtime.
When the summer starts it starts to feel warm,
Then we see the young cattle on the local farm.

Watch the bees collecting the pollen from the flowers
And the sun will stay warm for hours and hours.
Everything in bloom all happy and so bright,
And everything is relaxed in the warm night.

Your skin it might bronze in the warm sun,
But then the rain comes and our summer is done.
Autumn is here the leaves they fall from the trees,
You now need to wrap up from the cold breeze.

Everything goes brown all the flowers are dead,
And darker are the nights so it's earlier to bed.
As the rains come so heavy and so cold,
We all stay indoors the young and the old.

The winter then comes it's ever so sly,
We are watching the snow clouds that are up in the sky.
The snow it then covers every part of our town,
But it all looks so lovely in its little white gown.

The children they enjoy the snow so much,
But they still get cold from the snow that they touch.
I do hope that next year that spring isn't late
But we won't know for a while we will have to wait.

Angie Armstrong

HARMONY

Spring sings its song,
It flies through blue skies
On the back of nature,
Sunlight echoes the harmonies.

The glistening drainpipes,
Now empty of leaves and snow,
Outline the horizon of birth,
Re-birth, progress and evolution.

Throbbing energy bursts forth,
Happiness and joy,
Fills the atmosphere.
Lovers walk . . . lovers talk.

Birds caress the clouds,
Moulding their wings to the wind
And sing their first song,
Sweet sonnets of lyrical love.

Movement is abroad,
From the sleepy emergence of beasts,
To the flourishing flowers of the earth,
On whose stage, act one takes shape.

James F Kirk

CAMBRIDGE SNOW

One winter in 1927 snow fell on the city
quietly covering everything with white
billowing humps and comical lumps
lodging on college roofs, hooding pinnacles
and diamond crowning kingly statues.
Beyond, on the frozen backs, hollows filled
with purple shadows, stark trees
aged overnight their skeleton branches
creaking painfully, frost painted.
Distant horizons, mist brushed disappeared
heavy menacing snow clouds descended with a hiss.
The Cam flowed grey and sullenly swollen
under snow-covered bridges deserted and silent.
Moored punts disguised with pristine sheets
and pillows of snow swung with the stream
to dream of summer laughter and blue skies.
Gowned students, long scarf swaddled
scurried hurriedly back to chilly digs
with sluggishly smoking coal fires
to brew up tea, to toast muffins
and frozen toes swollen with chilblains.
Then out of the dusk towards the chapel lights
a crocodile of top-hatted choristers slither
chattering excitedly into Kings for Evensong.
High up in his room a homesick scholar
propped up a canvas against a biscuit tin
to paint a snowscape in sombre greys and whites
taking his spirit back to his familiar fens
to willows bent over dykes winter wise
and umber snow-filled murky mud flats
where biting winds whistle from endless skies
never thinking that seventy years on
a poet will write his painting as a song.

Audrey Willis

THE BEAUTY OF SPRING

The spring allows us to rejoice
To see the blossoming trees,
Or the shoot of that forgotten bulb
Waving in the breeze.
The bud upon the smallest flower
In a most unlikely patch,
Demonstrates a beauty that
No human hand could match.
Rivers also come to life
And rush with great elation,
The hillsides, too, burst forth with streams
To join the celebration.
Do you ever stop to think
That this was made to happen?
The great eternal promise of
That marvellous seasonal pattern.
As spring leads onto summer days
More wonders still are seen,
As flowers give a grand display
Amidst the plushest green.
The warmth of light of summertime
Gives all of us such pleasure,
And leaves us with a blessing far
Beyond all human measure.

Heather Sims

THE JOYS OF NATURE

The winter months, so hard, so cold,
Wrap up put your gloves on, face it, be bold,
Spring is coming, at last some sun,
Then come the showers, to make us more glum.

Summer arrives, holidays begin,
Out and about, take off on a whim,
The beach is calling, the long country walks,
Let's have a barbecue, break out the knives and forks.

Autumn appears, changes all around,
The trees are bare, their leaves on the ground,
Four seasons we have, they make up the year,
The forces of nature, are not really clear.

Dianne Brown

JUST DESSERTS

It's the 24th of May, nearly high mid-summer's day
And honestly you'd think it was November.
There's grey swirling mist about and you cannot cast a clout,
But years ago this time was *hot*, remember?

Now the howling gale and rain make fast rivers of the roads,
The temperature is 5 degrees or lower.
Our small world's gone quietly mad 'cos the climate's gone berserk -
Are the seasons changing faster now or slower?

Perhaps winter will be turning into summer
Or the autumn into spring - so what's the reason?
Well we've got our just desserts for the mess we've made on earth.
In the end there'll be one long drought ridden season.

Paddy Jupp

INFORMATION

We hope you have enjoyed reading this book - and that you will continue to enjoy it in the coming years.

If you like reading and writing poetry drop us a line, or give us a call, and we'll send you a free information pack.

Write to

Anchor Books Information
1-2 Wainman Road
Woodston
Peterborough
PE2 7BU